Set design by Tony Ferrieri

Photo by Ric Evans

(*Left to right*) Holli Hamilton, Jeffrey Howell, Laurie Klatscher, Tom J. Schaller in a scene from the City Theatre production of *Red Herring*.

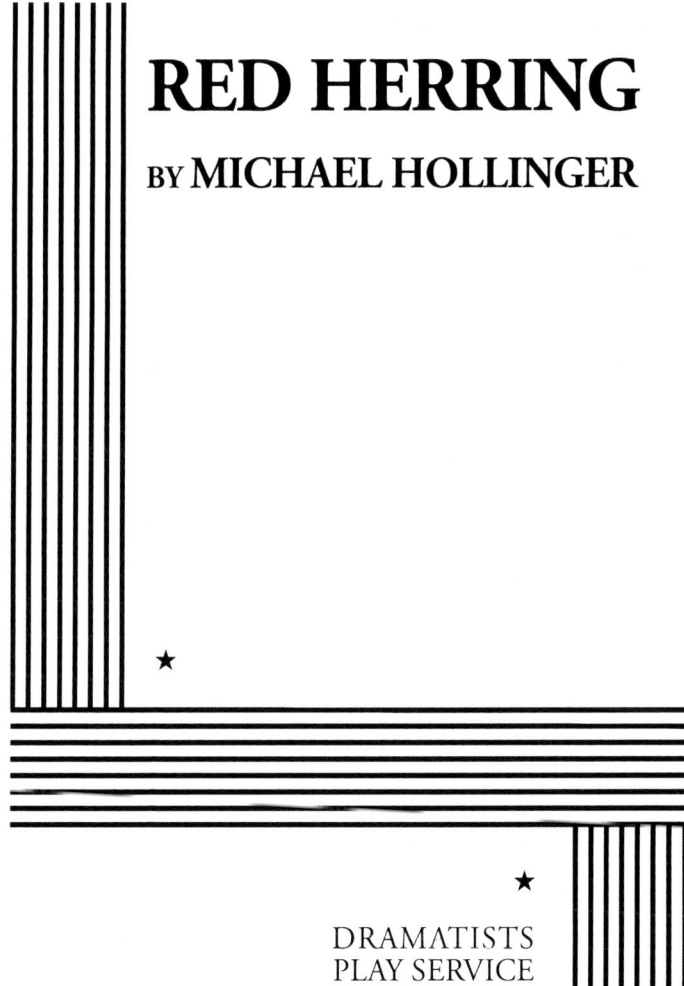

RED HERRING

BY MICHAEL HOLLINGER

DRAMATISTS
PLAY SERVICE
INC.

RED HERRING
Copyright © 2002 (Revised), Michael Hollinger
Copyright © 2000, Michael Hollinger
as an unpublished dramatic composition

All Rights Reserved

CAUTION: Professionals and amateurs are hereby warned that performance of RED HERRING is subject to payment of a royalty. It is fully protected under the copyright laws of the United States of America, and of all countries covered by the International Copyright Union (including the Dominion of Canada and the rest of the British Commonwealth), and of all countries covered by the Pan-American Copyright Convention, the Universal Copyright Convention, the Berne Convention, and of all countries with which the United States has reciprocal copyright relations. All rights, including without limitation professional/amateur stage rights, motion picture, recitation, lecturing, public reading, radio broadcasting, television, video or sound recording, all other forms of mechanical, electronic and digital reproduction, transmission and distribution, such as CD, DVD, the Internet, private and file-sharing networks, information storage and retrieval systems, photocopying, and the rights of translation into foreign languages are strictly reserved. Particular emphasis is placed upon the matter of readings, permission for which must be secured from the Author's agent in writing.

The English language stock and amateur stage performance rights in the United States, its territories, possessions and Canada for RED HERRING are controlled exclusively by DRAMATISTS PLAY SERVICE, INC., 440 Park Avenue South, New York, NY 10016. No professional or nonprofessional performance of the Play may be given without obtaining in advance the written permission of DRAMATISTS PLAY SERVICE, INC., and paying the requisite fee.

Inquiries concerning all other rights should be addressed to Harden-Curtis Associates, 214 West 29th Street, New York, NY 10001. Attn: Mary Harden.

SPECIAL NOTE
Anyone receiving permission to produce RED HERRING is required to give credit to the Author as sole and exclusive Author of the Play on the title page of all programs distributed in connection with performances of the Play and in all instances in which the title of the Play appears for purposes of advertising, publicizing or otherwise exploiting the Play and/or a production thereof. The name of the Author must appear on a separate line, in which no other name appears, immediately beneath the title and in size of type equal to 50% of the size of the largest, most prominent letter used for the title of the Play. No person, firm or entity may receive credit larger or more prominent than that accorded the Author. The following acknowledgment must appear on the title page in all programs distributed in connection with performances of the Play:

RED HERRING was originally produced
by Arden Theatre Company, Philadelphia, Pennsylvania.

for Meg, who shares my little dory

ACKNOWLEDGMENTS

My debt is great to my parents, who, with two broken hearts and one broken foot, finally got married in a police station. To Sara Garonzik, John Rea, Philadelphia Theatre Company, John Rando and cast for the play's first reading. To John Rando (again), Kate Maguire, Berkshire Theatre Festival, Terry Nolen and cast for the second reading/workshop. To Aaron Posner for advice and babysitting, and to the seemingly tireless Arden Theatre Company staff. To Terry Nolen (again and again), for working so hard to put on the stage what I've put on the page. And to Meg (again and again and again), without whom I would have no business writing a fable about marriage.

RED HERRING was originally produced by Arden Theatre Company (Terrence J. Nolen, Artistic Producing Director; Amy Murphy, Managing Director) in Philadelphia, Pennsylvania, on January 27, 2000. It was directed by Terrence J. Nolen; the set design was by James Kronzer; the lighting design was by James Leitner; the sound design was by James Sugg; the costume design was by Marla Jurglanis; and the production stage manager was Kristine A. Schipper. The cast was as follows:

MAGGIE PELLETIER	Jennifer Childs
FRANK KELLER	Scott Greer
LYNN McCARTHY	Abby Cucci
JAMES APPEL	Tony Braithwaite
MRS. KRAVITZ	Mary Martello
ANDREI BORCHEVSKY	Charles Antalosky

RED HERRING was produced by City Theatre (Marc Masterson, Producing Director; David Jobin, Managing Director) in Pittsburgh, Pennsylvania, on May 4, 2001. It was directed by Gregory Lehane; the set and properties design were by Tony Ferrieri; the lighting design was by Andrew David Ostrowski; the sound design was by Joe Pino; the costume design was by Lorraine Venberg; the voice and dialect coach was Don Wadsworth; and the production stage manager was Patti Kelly. The cast was as follows:

MAGGIE PELLETIER	Beth Bailey
FRANK KELLER	Tom J. Schaller
LYNN McCARTHY	Holli Hamilton
JAMES APPEL	Darren E. Focareta
MRS KRAVITZ	Laurie Klatscher
ANDREI BORCHEVSKY	Jeffrey Howell

CHARACTERS

Six actors play eighteen roles, as follows:

MAGGIE PELLETIER, mid-30s.

FRANK KELLER, mid-30s. This actor also plays: PRIEST, MAJOR HARTWELL, recorded voices as necessary.

LYNN McCARTHY, early 20s. This actress also plays: CLERK, recorded voices as necessary.

JAMES APPEL, early 20s. This actor also plays: WOODY, HARRY, BARTENDER, recorded voices as necessary.

MRS. KRAVITZ, late 40s, early 50s. This actress also plays: MRS. McCARTHY, MRS. VAN NOSTRAND, recorded voices as necessary.

ANDREI BORCHEVSKY, late 40s, early 50s. This actor also plays: PETEY, DR. KASDEN, HERBERT, CORPSE, recorded voices as necessary.

PLACE

Various suggested interiors and exteriors around Boston, in Wisconsin, and in the South Pacific.

TIME

The events of the play take place during one week (Wednesday–Tuesday), October 29–November 4, 1952.

NOTE: When one character begins speaking before the other has finished, the point of interruption is marked: "/."

SCENE BREAKDOWN

ACT ONE
(playing time: roughly one hour)

Scene 1: Wednesday morning, Maggie's apartment, Boston
Scene 2: Wednesday morning, McCarthy home, Wisconsin
Scene 3: Wednesday morning, Fish Pier, Boston
Scene 4: Wednesday afternoon, hotel room, Boston
Scene 5: Wednesday afternoon, McCarthy home, Wisconsin
Scene 6: Wednesday afternoon, morgue, Boston
Scene 7: Wednesday dusk, Fish Pier, Boston
Scene 8: Wednesday night, McCarthy home, Wisconsin
Scene 9: Thursday morning, Andrei's apartment, Boston
Scene 10: Thursday morning, airport, Wisconsin
Scene 11: Thursday evening, Maggie's and Mrs. Kravitz's apartments, Boston (split)
Scene 12: Friday afternoon, morgue, Boston
Scene 13: Friday afternoon, City Hall, Boston
Scene 14: Friday, dusk, bridal shop, Boston

ACT TWO
(playing time: under one hour)

Scene 15: Friday evening, Boston and the South Pacific (split)
Scene 16: Friday night, bar, Boston
Scene 17: Friday night, Fish Pier, Boston
Scene 18: Friday night, Kravitz apartment, Boston
Scene 19: Saturday morning, shipboard, South Pacific
Scene 20: Monday morning, hotel room, Boston
Scene 21: Monday evening, confessional, Boston
Scene 22: Tuesday evening, morgue, Boston
Scene 23: Tuesday evening, Mrs. Kravitz's and Andrei's apartments
Scene 24: Tuesday night, Fish Pier, Boston

NOTE: Setting elements should be as minimal as possible, in order to eliminate lengthy set changes and facilitate a swift, fluid pace. The above scene list is included for the benefit of producers, directors and designers. It should not be included in programs.

RED HERRING
a fable

ACT ONE

Scene 1

Before the play begins, a prominent billboard glows above the dark stage bearing an image of Winslow Homer's The Herring Net. *In the painting, two slickered figures labor over nets on a small fishing boat in the middle of an ominous sea. Over the image is emblazoned the brand name "Ogilby Kippers"; underneath, the slogan "Put a Fish in Your Pocket." As the billboard fades, lights rise dimly on a bed where Frank lies sleeping. After a moment, a door opens. Maggie enters furtively, wearing a single shoe. She clumps about, groping in the dark and under the bed. Suddenly Frank is up, brandishing the other shoe like a pistol.*

FRANK. Freeze, peg leg.
MAGGIE. Jumpin' Jesus!
FRANK. What do you think you're doin'?
MAGGIE. Tryin' not to wet myself. *(She turns to see him.)* There's that shoe. Where was it?
FRANK. Under my pillow.
MAGGIE. Frank …
FRANK. I'm sick of you sneakin' out on me.
MAGGIE. Well, duty calls. *(She reaches for the shoe, but he withholds it.)*
FRANK. All work, no play makes Jane a dull broad.
MAGGIE. You didn't think I was dull last night.

FRANK. Last night we were playin'. *(He pulls her in for a long kiss.)* But didn't anybody ever tell you it's rude to shout another man's name while makin' love?
MAGGIE. I figured "Oh Jesus" was exempt. *(She takes the shoe.)*
FRANK. Well if I catch this Jesus fella sendin' you flowers, he's gonna have to answer to me. *(Maggie sits and puts on the shoe with discomfort.)* Want to stop by the hotel later for an encore?
MAGGIE. Not sure your boss would approve of you makin' whoopie on the Bureau's dime …
FRANK. What J. Edgar doesn't know won't hurt him.
MAGGIE. Hoover knows everything. He's like Santa. *(She looks at the shoes on her feet.)* God I hate these shoes …
FRANK. Why don't you ditch 'em?
MAGGIE. They're regulation.
FRANK. Never known you to follow regulations.
MAGGIE. Lieutenant would love an excuse to put me back with the girls in Juvenile Aid. *(She stands.)* Besides, they give me an air of authority.
FRANK. They're givin' you bunions. *(She turns to exit.)* Listen, I wanted to ask you somethin' …
MAGGIE. Go ahead. *(But she immediately exits. Beat.)*
FRANK. I talked to this travel guy yesterday, over in Quincy? And he said — *(The phone rings. Maggie reenters, putting on her trench coat.)*
MAGGIE. He said what.
FRANK. He said he gets these special promotions — *(The phone rings.)*
MAGGIE. Hold that thought. *(She picks up the receiver.)* Yeah. *(Beat.)* Yeah? *(Pause.)* Where? *(Pause.)* I'll see you in twenty. *(She hangs up.)*
FRANK. Who was that?
MAGGIE. Jesus. Said he's comin' over to punch your lights out.
FRANK. Somebody died.
MAGGIE. So it would seem. Kid went fishin off Pier 17, reeled in a chunk of somebody's ear.
FRANK. What kind of bait was he usin'? *(She smiles.)*
MAGGIE. I'll see you tonight. *(She kisses him.)*
FRANK. Wait a second.

MAGGIE. What.
FRANK. Sit down.
MAGGIE. I can't …
FRANK. I gotta ask you somethin'.
MAGGIE. And I gotta run.
FRANK. Two minutes.
MAGGIE. Frank …
FRANK. Sit. *(He seats her on the bed and crosses to his trousers, which lie over the chair. Reaching into a pocket, Frank removes an envelope.)* Here. *(Beat.)*
MAGGIE. What's this?
FRANK. Anniversary present.
MAGGIE. What anniversary?
FRANK. Four months, seventeen days since you first called me an arrogant, pig-headed idiot.
MAGGIE. Seems like only yesterday.
FRANK. You said it yesterday, too. *(Maggie opens the envelope. She reads the tickets inside.)*
MAGGIE. "Tropicana Cruise Lines"…?
FRANK. Two tickets to Havana.
MAGGIE. What'd you do, win a rhumba contest?
FRANK. It's our honeymoon. *(Beat.)*
MAGGIE. Whose?
FRANK. Yours and mine.
MAGGIE. I thought gettin' married was a prerequisite.
FRANK. How 'bout that. *(She looks at him.)* This travel guy in Quincy says to me, "How'd you like to get on a slow boat to Cuba?" Some kind of special promotion or somethin'. I figure what the hell; then I figure, What The Hell. So. You wanna honeymoon with me in Havana? *(Beat.)*
MAGGIE. I don't know what to say …
FRANK. Say yes.
MAGGIE. I mean, this is all pretty quick …
FRANK. I know it's outta the blue, it's just … *(Beat.)* You been good for me. Got me off the bottle, blew the dust off my life. And I think I been good for you, too. *(Beat.)* We belong together. Like a pair of bum shoes. *(Pause.)*
MAGGIE. Where would we tie the knot?

FRANK. Why not on the boat? Get the captain to marry us. *(She hesitates.)* Come on, make an honest man outta me.
MAGGIE. I thought you were an honest man.
FRANK. I lied. What do you say? *(Pause.)*
MAGGIE. Not yet. *(She puts the tickets into his hands.)*
FRANK. I'm not gettin any better-lookin', if that's what you're waitin for.
MAGGIE. *(Getting up.)* It's not you, Frank ...
FRANK. You're not gettin any better-lookin' either ...
MAGGIE. Well, that was kind.
FRANK. I'm sorry; look —
MAGGIE. You know there's nobody else on my dance card. You know that, right? *(Pause. She starts to kiss him, but is interrupted by the phone ringing.)* All right, all right, I'm comin' already! *(She starts out.)* If that's Woody, can you tell him I'm on my way?
FRANK. What if it's Jesus? *(She stops, turns, smiles.)*
MAGGIE. Tell him I got a better offer. *(She exits. Frank looks down at the tickets in his hands. The phone keeps ringing. Blackout.)*

Scene 2

In darkness, the sound of a commercial jingle:

SINGERS.
"Put a fish in your pocket
Put a smile on your face
Pick up a can of Ogilby's
You can eat them anyplace!"
(Music continues underneath Announcer:)
ANNOUNCER. Ladies — is your family getting tired of the same old snacks? Next time, why not try a can of kippers in that lunch pail or briefcase. Ogilby's — tasty, nutritious herring from America's coastal waters. *(Lights up brightly on the living room of a suburban home. Lynn and James, both in their early twenties, sit fac-*

ing the television, from which comes the following:) We now return to the hearings of the Senate Internal Security Subcommittee.
McCARTHY. *(V.O.)* Mr. Chairman?
LYNN. *(Calling off.)* Mother!
CHAIRMAN. *(V.O.)* The Chair recognizes the senator from Wisconsin.
LYNN. *(As before.)* Daddy's on again!
McCARTHY. *(V.O.)* I'd like the witness to tell this committee where he spent the evening of December 31, 1949.
WITNESS. *(V.O.)* New Year's Eve?
McCARTHY. *(V.O.)* Was it or was it not at the home of Gordon Epstein, a former Communist?
WITNESS. *(V.O.)* Gordon? Gordon's not —
McCARTHY. You deny you spent the evening with Mr. Epstein?
WITNESS. *(V.O.)* Of course not; he invited my wife and I over —
McCARTHY. *(V.O.)* And at that gathering, did you or did you not lead participants in singing a Communist anthem?
WITNESS. "Communist" … ? I don't know any Communist —
McCARTHY. According to another guest, the witness quote "placed a lampshade on his head and began singing 'When the Red Red Robin Comes Bob-Bob-Bobbin' Along.'" Unquote. *(Beat.)*
WITNESS. I put a lampshade on my head? *(James, agitated, turns off the TV.)*
LYNN. James!
JAMES. You want to take a walk?
LYNN. A walk?
JAMES. Since the leaves are so pretty.
LYNN. Sure, after the hearings are over … *(She reaches to turn up the sound, but he takes her hand.)*
JAMES. I guess I just wanted a chance to be alone.
LYNN. We're alone.
JAMES. Without your mom in the next room.
LYNN. She won't bother us; she's on the phone with my Aunt Pidge. *(Beat.)*
JAMES. Well … all right. *(She reaches for the TV, but he grabs her hand again and reaches into his pocket.)*
LYNN. James?
JAMES. Here. *(He pulls out a small box and places it in her hand.)*

LYNN. What is … *(She opens it.)* Oh my goodness.
JAMES. Do you like it?
LYNN. It's beautiful!
JAMES. It's real.
LYNN. And so big…!
JAMES. That's what I asked for, "Gimme somethin' big," I said, " 'Cause I got a great big love for this little lady."
LYNN. Oh, Bunny … *(She kisses him on the cheek.)*
JAMES. Hey, don't waste that kiss on my cheek! *(She smiles and kisses him on the mouth.)*
LYNN. Let's go show Mother …
JAMES. Hold on — read the inscription.
LYNN. "One plus one equals … *(She turns the ring sideways.)* eight"?
JAMES. It's an infinity symbol.
LYNN. Oh!
JAMES. Because our love is infinite.
LYNN. I knew that didn't add up to eight.
JAMES. Let's see how it looks on you. *(He puts the ring on her finger.)*
LYNN. My heart's racing …
JAMES. You should have seen the jeweler's face when I said it was for Joe McCarthy's daughter.
LYNN. Did he say something mean?
JAMES. Heck no, you kidding? He gave me a discount! Though it was still pretty steep — you know, with all those carats … There!
LYNN. Oh, it's just perfect …
JAMES. So, you … really like it, then…?
LYNN. Of course, silly, you know I do.
JAMES. I mean, you know what I mean. Do you … will you…?
LYNN. Of course, silly, you know I will!
JAMES. Shazam!
LYNN. Now can we show Mother?
JAMES. Not so fast …
LYNN. Bunny!
JAMES. There's something I need to talk about first.
LYNN. I know what you're going to say.
JAMES. I don't think so.
LYNN. As long as you convert in time for the wedding, my parents will never be the wiser.

JAMES. Convert?
LYNN. Well you can't expect me to be Jewish, I'm Irish.
JAMES. Neither one of us should have to convert.
LYNN. You don't believe in God as it is, what difference would it make to be Catholic?
JAMES. Let's not get into this now. I really need to tell you something.
LYNN. Okay, okay, then tell me. *(Beat.)*
JAMES. You'll really marry me?
LYNN. Didn't I just say so?
JAMES. I know, but ... *(Beat.)*
LYNN. But what, what do you have to tell me?
JAMES. Um, this should come as a bit of a surprise ...
LYNN. If it's anything like your last surprise, it's okay by me. What is it? *(Beat.)* James? *(Beat.)*
JAMES. I'm a spy. *(Pause.)*
LYNN. Excuse me?
JAMES. I said I'm a —
LYNN. What do you mean you're a spy?
JAMES. I mean I'm a Soviet spy. *(Pause.)*
LYNN. So that's what you do all the time in New Mexico?
JAMES. Not ... all the time, but —
LYNN. I've been telling everyone you're a physicist.
JAMES. Well, I am —
LYNN. But you're really a spy?
JAMES. Not so loud ...
LYNN. Bunny, that is so glamorous ... *(Pause.)*
JAMES. You mean you don't mind?
LYNN. Are you kidding? Wait'll I tell Daddy ...
JAMES. Uh, you can't tell your father.
LYNN. Why not?
JAMES. 'Cause it's a secret.
LYNN. Well you told me.
JAMES. You're my fiancée.
LYNN. Where do you find them?
JAMES. Find what?
LYNN. Soviets. In the desert.
JAMES. Uh ...

LYNN. They should send you to Moscow, more of them there;
JAMES. Well —
LYNN. ... though I wouldn't want to move to Moscow, would you? So cold and gloomy ...
JAMES. I don't spy on Soviets.
LYNN. You've said New Mexico's nice, though ...
JAMES. Did you hear me?
LYNN. What.
JAMES. I said I don't spy on Soviets. *(Beat.)*
LYNN. I don't understand.
JAMES. I don't spy *on* them. I spy for them. *(Pause.)*
LYNN. You mean you're a Commie?
JAMES. Well, I don't go to meetings, but —
LYNN. Oh my God, you're a Commie!
JAMES. Shhh ...
LYNN. COMMIE!
JAMES. Lynn ...
LYNN. COMMIE! *(James touches his fingers to her lips just as Mrs. McCarthy calls from offstage:)*
MRS. McCARTHY. *(O.S.)* Lynn, what's the matter? Did you call Mommy?
JAMES. Uh, it's nothing, Mrs. McCarthy. We're just ... playing Scrabble.
MRS. McCARTHY. *(O.S.)* Scrabble?
JAMES. "Oh, look — triple word score ... "
MRS. McCARTHY. *(O.S.)* Well, keep it down, will you? Aunt Pidge is calling all the way from Des Moines. *(James removes his hand from Lynn's lips; Lynn appears terrified.)*
JAMES. Sorry. I didn't mean to drop it on you like that.
LYNN. Why are you a Commie?
JAMES. I'm not —
LYNN. You just told me —
JAMES. *I'm not a Commie,* I just think ... *(He gathers his thoughts.)* Down there in the desert, we're building a bomb. A super-bomb, so powerful no nation in the world should keep it to themselves, even us. So, I've been passing information to the Russians so they can build one for themselves.
LYNN. I thought they already had the Bomb.

JAMES. The atom bomb's only a fission bomb — neutrons splitting other atoms. But the Super is a fusion bomb — neutrons joining other atoms.
LYNN. So this one will kill people deader than the other?
JAMES. The point is not to kill anyone, the point — if only one man has a gun, then everyone else is in danger. But if two men each have a gun, there's a balance of power, so we all stay safe.
LYNN. Unless they both decide to shoot us. *(James considers this wisdom for a second, then brushes it aside:)*
JAMES. Look, I don't want to argue; I want you to be my wife. So we'll never have to argue again.
LYNN. All right, but you have to stop this spy business.
JAMES. I will.
LYNN. Promise.
JAMES. I promise.
LYNN. Good. *(They kiss.)*
JAMES. ... after I deliver this one last package —
LYNN. James!
JAMES. ... the last set of blueprints before we test.
LYNN. No.
JAMES. It's simple:
LYNN. I said no.
JAMES. ... a ten-second hand-off in Boston next Friday.
LYNN. You won't even be in the country by then.
JAMES. I know.
LYNN. You'll be in the middle of the ocean!
JAMES. I know.
LYNN. Then how do you expect to deliver a package in Bost*oh God you want me to do it ...*
JAMES. It'll be so easy.
LYNN. Oh God, James ...
JAMES. Just tell your mom you're visiting friends at Radcliffe ...
LYNN. I can't believe this ...
JAMES. It's totally anonymous.
LYNN. First you tell me you're a Commie ...
JAMES. I'm not a —
LYNN. Then you want me to be a Commie ...
JAMES. I'm only asking you —

LYNN. Commie!
JAMES. Don't call me that.
LYNN. Commie!
JAMES. Shh — Lynn!
LYNN. COMMIE COMMIE COMMIE COMMIE COMMIE — *(James moves swiftly behind Lynn, covering her mouth with his right hand.)*
MRS. McCARTHY. *(O.S.)* Children, please, do I have to take away the Scrabble bo — *(She enters, holding a telephone receiver.)* Oh!
JAMES. Mrs. McCarthy …
MRS. McCARTHY. Oh my …
JAMES. Mrs. McCarthy — I've just asked your daughter for her hand in marriage … *(Hand still on her mouth, James thrusts out Lynn's left hand to display the ring.)* … and she's agreed to marry me!
MRS. McCARTHY. Really? *(Lynn looks over at James, then back at her mother. She nods.)* Well, that's wonderful news! Did you hear that, Pidge? My little baby's all grown up and ready to be a wife! *(James and Lynn look at each other. Blackout.)*

Scene 3

Lights rise on a fishing pier in Boston. Maggie kneels beside a body covered with a cloth; only the left hand protrudes, lying atop the body. She looks through a few small items in her hand. Woody, a crime photographer, occasionally takes flash photos — FWOOSH! — of the covered body.

WOODY. Oh, yeah, that's it — plenty of luminance. Hold it … *(FWOOSH!)* Nice. What'd his pockets turn up?
MAGGIE. Not much. A Beantown library card, expired …
WOODY. That fits.
MAGGIE. Two Tums, thirty-six cents in change.
WOODY. Guess the killer whacked him for his wallet.

MAGGIE. This guy wasn't robbed.
WOODY. How do you know?
MAGGIE. Nobody who'd kill for cash would leave behind that ring.
WOODY. This is why *you* carry the badge. *(Looking through the viewfinder.)* Ooh, very optical-visual … *(FWOOSH!)*
MAGGIE. I thought you were all done here.
WOODY. I'm finishin up a roll: a smooth-gamma tonal study.
MAGGIE. I'll take your word for it. *(She slips the small items into a handkerchief and pockets them.)*
WOODY. Hey, photography's an art, you know. Ever hear of Henry Cartier-Bresson?
MAGGIE. He that fat magician on Sullivan last week?
WOODY. No, he's French. Wrote a whole book about capturing the Decisive Moment. So I don't care what those snooty sketch guys down at the station say — I am an artist. *(Looking through the viewfinder.)* Beautiful juxtaposition … *(FWOOSH!)*
MAGGIE. Looks like we got company. *(Maggie pulls out a notepad and pen. Mrs. Kravitz enters in housecoat and slippers, her hair in curlers.)*
MRS. KRAVITZ. A cop asked me to identify a body.
MAGGIE. You the super?
MRS. KRAVITZ. You the stenographer?
MAGGIE. *(Flashing her badge.)* Detective Pelletier, ma'am. This is Woody Coyle …
WOODY. *(Looking at Mrs. Kravitz through the viewfinder.)* Love your gradiant …
MAGGIE. He's an artist.
MRS. KRAVITZ. Hey — you're that lady copy, aren't you?
MAGGIE. Was it the skirt that tipped you off?
MRS. KRAVITZ. I read about you in *True Detective.*
MAGGIE. "The Flatfoot in Heels" …
MRS. KRAVITZ. Right!
MAGGIE. Creative journalism. I appreciate your givin' us a positive ID, Mrs…?
MRS. KRAVITZ. Kravitz, Florence Kravitz, Kravitz with a "K."
MAGGIE. Have you ever seen a lifeless body before?
MRS. KRAVITZ. My ex-husband, every night of our marriage. *(FWOOSH!)*

MAGGIE. Let me rephrase the question. *(She lifts the cloth so Mrs. Kravitz can see the body.)* Ever seen one of your own tenants drowned in a cardigan, dickey, and two-tone shoes? *(Beat.)*
MRS. KRAVITZ. No, this is a first.
MAGGIE. I'd hate to think it was a weekly event. *(She covers the body again.)* So: What can you tell me about the stiff with the dickey?
MRS. KRAVITZ. Quiet type. Took the room next to mine. Sometimes he brought me fish.
MAGGIE. Fish?
MRS. KRAVITZ. He captained a seiner for Ogilby's. You ever cook with herring?
MAGGIE. I don't cook.
MRS. KRAVITZ. Very versatile fish.
WOODY. *(To Mrs. Kravitz.)* Oh yeah. My mother makes a red sauce with herring, you'd swear you're eatin' veal scallopini. *(Maggie just looks at him, then turns back to Mrs. Kravitz.)*
MAGGIE. Did he mention a missus?
MRS. KRAVITZ. A missus?
MAGGIE. *(Indicating the hand with the wedding ring.)* Whoever's got the mate to this.
MRS. KRAVITZ. She's somewhere back in the Old Country.
MAGGIE. How 'bout a mistress in the new one?
MRS. KRAVITZ. Isn't that personal?
MAGGIE. Not if she killed him.
MRS. KRAVITZ. What if she didn't?
MAGGIE. *(Making a note.)* So there was a mistress — do you know her name?
MRS. KRAVITZ. I'd rather show some respect for the dead.
MAGGIE. This is how I show respect. Her name?
MRS. KRAVITZ. What about you, you married?
MAGGIE. That is personal.
MRS. KRAVITZ. Mistress, huh? *(FWOOSH!)* What's a nice girl like you doin' wearin' a holster instead of a wedding ring?
MAGGIE. Maybe I like a good mystery.
MRS. KRAVITZ. Ha! Marriage is a mystery. Why two young, attractive people, full of potential, would promise to love each other at their *worst?* There's a mystery'd make Dashiell Hammett

look like a hack.
MAGGIE. About that mistress...? *(Pause.)*
MRS. KRAVITZ. The man was unusually devoted to his wife. I can't imagine a mistress who'd put up with it. *(Maggie makes a note.)* And you, still waitin' for Mr. Right?
MAGGIE. As it happens, I already found him.
MRS. KRAVITZ. Which one of you's got cold feet?
WOODY. Maggie's got a case to unravel before she ties the knot. *(Woody winks at Maggie, who glares back.)*
MRS. KRAVITZ. *(To Maggie.)* You don't say?
WOODY. Ever hear of Moby Dick?
MAGGIE. Woody ...
MRS. KRAVITZ. Like the book?
WOODY. Like the Big Fish that got away. Goes by a dozen different names: Zoltan Toth, Lester Tarabian, Sam Schmidt ... After a hit, he gets a new face, and POOF!
MAGGIE. You musta missed it in *True Detective*. Now —
MRS. KRAVITZ. Wait — this the one with the Mercury dimes?
WOODY. Bingo.
MRS. KRAVITZ. Like a signature at the crime scene.
MAGGIE. May I remind you that this is a crime scene, and this guy's killer needs catchin', too. *(She looks pointedly at Woody, who backs off.)* Mrs. Kravitz: Despite the occasional gift of herring, your tenant lied to you.
MRS. KRAVITZ. Lied?
MAGGIE. *(Lifting the hand again.)* No cuts, callouses, dirt under the nails ... He may have been a dentist, but he wasn't a waterman.
MRS. KRAVITZ. Why would he lie?
MAGGIE. That's the sixty-four-dollar question. You'll be at your building all day?
MRS. KRAVITZ. I got living tenants, too, you know.
MAGGIE. I'll want to talk to all of 'em, check out his room, his belongings. Make sure the door stays locked till I get there.
WOODY. Uh, Maggie? *(She turns to him.)* Could you and Mrs. Kravitz move in a little bit? *(He motions for them to come together behind the body.)*
MAGGIE. What?
WOODY. I got one shot left.

MRS. KRAVITZ. My hair's not done.
WOODY. I'm goin' for veritay.
MAGGIE. Woody … *(Mrs. Kravitz moves in; Woody looks through his viewfinder.)*
WOODY. That's it — little closer. *(Mrs. Kravitz moves next to Maggie.)* Perfect. Now — say "fromage"! *(Mrs. Kravitz puts her arm around Maggie, pulls her close, and smiles grotesquely. Maggie looks on. FWOOSH! Blackout.)*

Scene 4

A hotel room. Petey, headphones around his neck, is seated on a bed, beside which sits a table with a reel-to-reel tape recorder and telephone. Frank, wearing an overcoat and holding a sheet of paper, has just entered from outside.

FRANK. Hold on to your socks.
PETEY. How come?
FRANK. 'Cause I got Big News.
PETEY. What?
FRANK. Three guesses.
PETEY. Maggie said yes! *(Beat.)*
FRANK. No.
PETEY. She said no?
FRANK. That's not the Big News.
PETEY. Did you give her the tickets? *(Frank pulls the ticket envelope out and tosses it on the bed.)*
FRANK. Maybe she just needs time to think it over.
PETEY. No. Gettin' hitched is one of those decisions you should make without thinkin' too much — like gettin' tattooed. You wander into the wrong side of town, get drunk, pay some lowlife to do the deed, then live with your mistake the rest of your life.
FRANK. You got one guess left.
PETEY. I don't know — tell me. *(Frank sits on the edge of the bed*

and holds up the piece of paper.)
FRANK. I think I found our spy.
PETEY. Get outta here — who?
FRANK. Borchevsky.
PETEY. The fisherman? *(Frank nods.)* How do you know?
FRANK. I checked the harbor logs. The morning after every meeting, Borchevsky goes to sea. *(Referring to the paper:)* January seventh, January eighth; April nineteenth, April twentieth; July thirtieth, July thirty-first.
PETEY. That means we're comin up on another …
FRANK. Which we gotta intercept. If we can't plug the leak at Los Alamos, we gotta cork it here.
PETEY. *(Checking his watch.)* Then we better hump it to the office, talk with the chief.
FRANK. Let's go. *(Petey grabs his coat; they prepare to leave. There is a knock at the door. Both men freeze.)* Who is it?
MAGGIE. *(O.S.)* Special Delivery for Mr. Keller. *(Frank and Petey exchange a glance.)*
FRANK. How special?
MAGGIE. *(O.S.)* That femme fatale you ordered. *(Frank opens the door.)*
FRANK. Is it COD? I'm a little short.
MAGGIE. You'll grow. *(She kisses him a good long one.)*
PETEY. Please, don't be discreet on my account.
MAGGIE. *(Moving into the room.)* Hey, Pete.
PETEY. Maggie.
MAGGIE *(To Frank.)* Pay phone on the pier was busted, can I use yours? *(She picks up the phone.)*
FRANK. We're just headin out …
MAGGIE. Take me a minute.
PETEY. What's your hurry?
MAGGIE. I need an autopsy.
PETEY. No kiddin' — you look fine to me. *(Maggie gives him a look.)*
MAGGIE. *(On phone.)* Hilltop 6572. *(Pause.)* Harry — Maggie. Listen, can you cut me a body this afternoon? *(Beat.)* I know, believe me, I know, but we gotta move fast on this one. *(Beat.)* You're a Georgia peach, Harry. *(She hangs up.)* Where you boys off to?

FRANK. Headquarters, take a meeting with the boss.
MAGGIE. Big News?
PETEY. Frank's got a lead on our spy.
MAGGIE. That's my G-man. Who is it?
FRANK. Russian fisherman named Borchevsky. *(Beat.)*
MAGGIE. Borchevsky?
PETEY. Yeah, why?
MAGGIE. Andrei Borchevsky, fishes for Ogilby's?
FRANK. You know him? *(Beat.)*
MAGGIE. He's my dead guy. *(Frank and Petey look at each other. Blackout.)*

Scene 5

The McCarthy home. Mrs. McCarthy measures oats into a mixing bowl.

LYNN. Mother …
MRS. McCARTHY. Yes dear?
LYNN. You can stop now.
MRS. McCARTHY. All right. *(She continues.)*
LYNN. Did you hear me?
MRS. McCARTHY. What was that?
LYNN. Stop baking. *(Lynn wrests the box of oats from her hands.)*
MRS. McCARTHY. I can't.
LYNN. You've been baking for hours — we'll never eat them all!
MRS. McCARTHY. I'll send some down to your father in Washington. He works up such an appetite fighting the forces of evil.
LYNN. Can't we just talk for a minute?
MRS. McCARTHY. Why of course, dear … *(She finally notices her daughter.)* What's the matter? You don't look like a girl who just put a great big diamond on her finger.
LYNN. I guess I'm a little confused, that's all.
MRS. McCARTHY. Why would you feel confused? Don't you

love him?
LYNN. Well, sure, but ...
MRS. McCARTHY. But what? *(Pause.)*
LYNN. Did Daddy ever ask you to do something you felt awkward about?
MRS. McCARTHY. Oh yes, dear.
LYNN. Really?
MRS. McCARTHY. Many times. But I told him if he wanted that he'd have to find some Chinese call girl, because no Christian wife would do it. *(Beat.)*
LYNN. Oh!
MRS. McCARTHY. Why, did James ask you to do something?
LYNN. Well, yeah, but nothing like that.
MRS. McCARTHY. Was it a number? *(Beat.)*
LYNN. A number?
MRS. McCARTHY. Or did it involve a pair of handcuffs and a ripe tomato?
LYNN. No! No ... handcuffs.
MRS. McCARTHY. Thank heaven! Then what made you feel awkward?
LYNN. Well ... this morning, after he proposed, he told me something about himself that ... kind of took me by surprise.
MRS. McCARTHY. What was that?
LYNN. He said he ... he's ...
MRS. McCARTHY. He's what, dear?
LYNN. He's ... *(She chickens out.)* not Catholic. *(Beat.)*
MRS. McCARTHY. Oh!
LYNN. Yeah. *(Pause. Mrs. McCarthy waits for her to continue. When she does not:)*
MRS. McCARTHY. What is he?
LYNN. What do you mean?
MRS. McCARTHY. If he's not Catholic.
LYNN. Oh. Uh ... *(Seeing the box of oats in her hand:)* Quaker.
MRS. McCARTHY. Really?
LYNN. Uh-huh.
MRS. McCARTHY. Quaker ...
LYNN. Yeah.
MRS. McCARTHY. Huh. *(Pause. Trying to find a positive angle:)*

Dick Nixon's Quaker.
LYNN. Is he?
MRS. McCARTHY. Oh yes. He's a very well-known Quaker.
LYNN. Well, then, how bad could they be?
MRS. McCARTHY. Your Aunt Pidge told me she visited a Quaker mass once in Philadelphia.
LYNN. Really?
MRS. McCARTHY. I think it's a tourist thing there. Like the Amish.
LYNN. What did she think?
MRS. McCARTHY. Oh, it sounded just awful. When the priest never showed up, the whole congregation just sat there for an hour.
LYNN. Well, we certainly shouldn't hold that against James.
MRS. McCARTHY. Of course not, dear. To tell you the truth, I was kind of relieved when you said he was Quaker.
LYNN. Relieved?
MRS. McCARTHY. *(Confidentially.)* I was afraid you were going to say he's Jewish! *(She laughs a little too hard. Lynn laughs uncomfortably.)*

Scene 6

The morgue. Maggie and Frank stand over the body, lying face up on a gurney, covered with a white cloth. Harry, a Georgia-accented coroner, wears a variety of "I Like Ike" buttons, an Ike bow tie, and carries Ike bubble-gum cigars in his lab coat pocket. He perkily recreates the autopsy process as Maggie examines autopsy notes on a clipboard.

HARRY. Okay, let's talk turkey: First we made a Y-incision and removed the chest plate. Took out the heart, weighed it, cut it up. Pulled out the lungs, weighed 'em, cut 'em up. Yanked out the liver, the spleen, kidneys, bowels, chopped them up. Sawed open the skull, popped out the brain, sliced and diced. Dissected the neck, the spinal column, spinal cord —

MAGGIE. You can jump to the verdict.
HARRY. This man is dead.
FRANK. Hold the front page.
MAGGIE. This says no water in the lungs, or the stomach ...
FRANK. *(To Harry.)* Does that mean he didn't drown?
HARRY. The brain did show signs of swellin'; flattenin' of the surface ...
MAGGIE. *(Reading.)* "Petechial hemmorhages in the eyes ... "
HARRY. But these only indicate a lack of oxygen. Could be a dozen different causes. You like Ike?
MAGGIE. *(Looking up.)* Huh?
FRANK. I like Ike.
HARRY. Then tell the world, my friend. *(He indicates his collection.)* I got buttons, I got bow ties, I got bubble-gum cigars ...
MAGGIE. I gather you like Ike.
HARRY. I love Ike. Come next week we kick the New Dealers out of the White House.
MAGGIE. *(Back to the clipboard.)* Were you able to get any prints?
HARRY. His fingers were pruney from the water, but we injected oil and took all ten. They're already on their way to Washington. So, you gonna tell me why the Bureau's involved, or do I have to wait till I read it in the *Herald*? *(Frank looks to Maggie.)*
MAGGIE. He's okay.
FRANK. Borchevsky was part of a spy ring trafficking in secret weapons information. *(Harry whistles.)*
HARRY. How big's the ring?
FRANK. Three guys that we know of. An unidentified mole at Los Alamos — let's say you — steals blueprints *(He takes a bubble-gum cigar.)* and brings them to Hermes — that's me. *(He tucks the cigar into his own upper pocket.)*
HARRY. "Hermes"?
MAGGIE. It's a code name: "The Messenger."
FRANK. Hermes sets up meetings, collects the cash. And finally gets the goods to Borchevsky, *(He places the cigar on top of the corpse.)* who delivers it to the Reds in international waters.
HARRY. Not anymore he doesn't. *(He takes back the cigar.)*
MAGGIE. What's this under Stomach Contents — "1934 D"?
HARRY. Ah — I was savin' the best for last. We won't know if it

was poisoned till we test for toxins ...
MAGGIE. If what was poisoned?
HARRY. But right in the middle of his dinner was this: *(He holds up a small coin. Maggie is dumbstruck. Pause.)*
FRANK. A Mercury dime ...
HARRY. Smooth as a button. *(Maggie takes the coin, mesmerized. To Frank:)* I still can't get used to the new ones. Just 'cause my daddy was a Democrat doesn't mean I gotta carry FDR in my pants.
FRANK. Maggie?
MAGGIE. *(Still staring at the coin.)* Huh?
FRANK. What do you think? *(Beat. She clenches the coin in her fist.)*
MAGGIE. I think it's time to sharpen my harpoon ... *(Blackout.)*

Scene 7

The fish pier. Dusk. Mrs. Kravitz, bundled up, looks offstage, from where we hear the sounds of a boat engine. After a few moments, Andrei's boat eases into port. Mrs. Kravitz looks around edgily. Andrei, a slickered, middle-aged fisherman, disembarks.

MRS. KRAVITZ. Andrei.
ANDREI. *(Peering to see her clearly.)* Mrs. Kravitz...?
MRS. KRAVITZ. It's me.
ANDREI. *(Elated.)* Mrs. Kravitz! *(Andrei quickly ties up the boat and joins her on the dock.)* What are you doing here? *(He looks around.)*
MRS. KRAVITZ. I wanted to welcome you home.
ANDREI. Oh, Mrs. Kravitz ... *(He takes her hands.)*
MRS. KRAVITZ. Call me Florence.
ANDREI. Every night I am thinking of you, kissing your picture, *(He kisses her hands.)* praying that one day soon we can — *(Noting her agitation.)* What is it? Something has happened ...
MRS. KRAVITZ. I got some good news and some bad. *(Beat.)*

ANDREI. About Olga? *(Beat.)*
MRS. KRAVITZ. About Nathan.
ANDREI. Nathan? *(Mrs. Kravitz nods.)* He has hurt you?
MRS. KRAVITZ. No ...
ANDREI. I will kill him ...
MRS. KRAVITZ. Andrei ...
ANDREI. If he puts a finger, I swear I will —
MRS. KRAVITZ. I already did. *(Beat.)*
ANDREI. What?
MRS. KRAVITZ. Took care of Nathan.
ANDREI. "Took care" ... ?
MRS. KRAVITZ. I had to, it was either him or us.
ANDREI. *(With increasing horror.)* You mean...?
MRS. KRAVITZ. I found things, Andrei ...
ANDREI. Oh my God ...
MRS. KRAVITZ. ... scary things. You woulda done the same.
ANDREI. Mrs. Kravitz ...
MRS. KRAVITZ. Listen —
ANDREI. ... I cannot believe —
MRS. KRAVITZ. *Listen to me.*
ANDREI. Yes, what? What is it? *(Beat.)*
MRS. KRAVITZ. You haven't heard the bad news yet. *(Pause.)*
ANDREI. Tell me. *(Beat.)*
MRS. KRAVITZ. You're the one who's dead. *(Beat.)*
ANDREI. What?
MRS. KRAVITZ. I'm sorry.
ANDREI. What do you mean —
MRS. KRAVITZ. I had no choice.
ANDREI. I don't under — *(Pause.)* No, Mrs. Kravitz ...
MRS. KRAVITZ. If it coulda been any different —
ANDREI. No, I cannot be dead ...
MRS. KRAVITZ. Believe me, you're deader than radio. They found you this morning off Pier 17. *(Long pause. Andrei considers this.)* I got you a new LP. *(She produces it from beneath her coat and hands it to him.)* South Pacific — the one with "Some Enchanted Evening." *(He nods vaguely. Pause.)*
ANDREI. What about Olga?
MRS. KRAVITZ. Forget about Olga.

ANDREI. She is still my wife.
MRS. KRAVITZ. No. Now she's your widow. Now we're both widows. *(Andrei looks at her. She closes his coat against the cold.)* Look at it this way: We're halfway there ... *(He looks down at the LP.)* I made some chowder. We'll draw a hot bath, put on your LP. Make some music of our own ... *(She touches his face gently, then pulls away.)* Don't go near your apartment. Come up the fire escape. I'll leave the window open. *(She turns to go.)*
ANDREI. What about my catch?
MRS. KRAVITZ. *(Turning back.)* Dump it.
ANDREI. I have two thousand pounds of herring on that boat!
MRS. KRAVITZ. Then you'll have to put it back where you found it. Dead men don't fish. *(Blackout.)*

Scene 8

McCarthy home. Night. James is asleep in bed as Lynn opens the door.

LYNN. *(Whispering.)* James? *(Pause.)* James? *(Pause. She gives his shoulder a little shake.)* Bunny? *(Pause. She pokes at him hard.)* James.
JAMES. HUH!
LYNN. Shhh ...
JAMES. What, what is it?
LYNN. Did I wake you? *(Beat.)*
JAMES. What?
LYNN. Were you asleep?
JAMES. What are you doing here?
LYNN. I heard you scream.
JAMES. Of course I screamed, you woke me up!
LYNN. Shhh — no, before I came in; I heard you call my name.
JAMES. I did?
LYNN. Maybe I just wanted you to.
JAMES. I was ... wow.

LYNN. What.
JAMES. Oh wow ...
LYNN. What is it?
JAMES. I had this crazy dream ...
LYNN. So did I!
JAMES. You did?
LYNN. Yes!
JAMES. On the boat?
LYNN. Yes! You were lying naked on the bottom of a rowboat and I was on top of you, pulling at the oars, back and forth, and ... *(James just looks at her.)* Was that it? *(Beat.)*
JAMES. No ... *(Beat.)*
LYNN. Oh. *(Beat.)* Um ... what was your dream? *(It takes James a moment to dislodge the previous image. Then he begins to revisit his own dream:)*
JAMES. I was standing on some kind of ship with Dr. Kasden and Major Hartwell. And we're waiting for the bomb test — there's the countdown: ten ... nine ... eight ... And when I look toward the island, I see something splashing in the water.
LYNN. What?
JAMES. Like a ... porpoise or something. But when I look closer, I realize it's you.
LYNN. Me?
JAMES. And you're really going, splashing around —
LYNN. You mistook me for a porpoise?
JAMES. It was a dream! *(He envisions the dream again:)* And I realize, if I don't stop the countdown, you're just going to be vaporized. But I can't speak, I can't even move, and when I look back in the water, I see you've disappeared beneath the waves. Only it's not water anymore — it's blood.
LYNN. Oh, Bunny.
JAMES. Then this bright light hit my face and I woke up.
LYNN. Wow. *(Beat.)* I like my dream better.
JAMES. Me too. *(Pause.)*
LYNN. I'm cold. Can I get in bed with you?
JAMES. Oh — sure. *(Lynn sits next to James; he puts his arm around her. Pause.)*
LYNN. James?

JAMES. Yeah, Bunny?
LYNN. How would you feel about being Quaker? *(Beat.)*
JAMES. Quaker?
LYNN. Like the religion.
JAMES. Why would I want to be Quaker?
LYNN. Lots of respectable people are Quaker.
JAMES. Wait:
LYNN. Dick Nixon's Quaker.
JAMES. Did you tell your mother I was Quaker?
LYNN. It's not like I'm asking you to be Mormon.
JAMES. Lynn!
LYNN. If only you believed in God —
JAMES. *(For the hundredth time.)* I believe in physics and physics is God.
LYNN. Shh …
JAMES. How much closer to God can you get than matter and energy?
LYNN. My mother will hear you!
JAMES. I want to open the atom and look in the eye of God, behold — *(Lynn kisses James impulsively and for a long time. Finally, they disengage.)* Wow! What was that for?
LYNN. I want you, James.
JAMES. Oh me too, baby lamb; soon as we're married —
LYNN. Tonight. *(Beat.)*
JAMES. Tonight?
LYNN. Well, you're leaving tomorrow and I won't see you for weeks …
JAMES. Are you sure?
LYNN. Unless I hop a plane for the Marshall Islands, but —
JAMES. I mean, are you sure you want to?
LYNN. Oh, yeah. *(Pause.)*
JAMES. *(This is too good to be true.)* Shazam! *(They kiss again, more enthusiastically. Lynn pulls away.)*
LYNN. Just tell me one thing: Are you a virgin?
JAMES. Am I a virgin?
LYNN. That's what I'm asking.
JAMES. Yes, of course. *(She exhales.)*
LYNN. Okay;

JAMES. What did you think, we'd be apart five months —
LYNN. Because I'm not. *(Beat.)*
JAMES. What?
LYNN. I'm not. A virgin. *(Pause.)*
JAMES. Oh ...
LYNN. I mean, I'm almost a virgin, I certainly was, up until this summer, but ... *(Beat.)*
JAMES. But?
LYNN. But I met this person and he ... we ...
JAMES. Wow.
LYNN. Yeah. *(Pause.)*
JAMES. It wasn't in a rowboat, was it?
LYNN. Oh, no, that was just a dream. *(James nods thoughtfully. Pause.)*
JAMES. Where was it then?
LYNN. James ...
JAMES. It's a reasonable question. *(Beat. Lynn sighs.)*
LYNN. In the Cambridge Roxy. During *The Prisoner of Zenda*. *(Pause.)*
JAMES. I heard that was good.
LYNN. Oh God, it was amazing! I mean, yeah, it was okay. *(Pause.)*
JAMES. Was it anyone I know?
LYNN. Well, Stewart Granger and Deborah Kerr ...
JAMES. That's not what I mean.
LYNN. James ...
JAMES. What?
LYNN. You're embarrassing me.
JAMES. Don't I have a right to know?
LYNN. *(Getting up.)* It's late ...
JAMES. Don't go ...
LYNN. I shouldn't have woken you ...
JAMES. Lynn:
LYNN. We'll talk in the morning.
JAMES. I want to get to the bottom of this! *(Beat.)*
LYNN. Now you sound just like my father ...
JAMES. I'm sorry.
LYNN. This isn't easy for me.
JAMES. Come here.

LYNN. I mean, it's not like I'm proud of it.
JAMES. Sit down.
LYNN. I just thought you should know.
JAMES. And I appreciate it, I do. *(Beat.)* Just tell me one thing …
LYNN. James …
JAMES. One thing.
LYNN. What.
JAMES. Tell me it wasn't Skip Vanderhooven.
LYNN. It wasn't Skip Vanderhooven.
JAMES. Thank god. *(Beat.)*
LYNN. Who's Skip Vanderhooven?
JAMES. My old lab partner. *(Beat.)*
LYNN. Oh.
JAMES. What a letch.
LYNN. Um …
JAMES. Always sleeping around …
LYNN. James?
JAMES. And the way he used to look at you, like some …
LYNN. It was him.
JAMES. … juicy piece of — what?
LYNN. It was Skip Vanderhooven.
JAMES. You just said it wasn't.
LYNN. That was before I knew his name.
JAMES. You gave the most intimate part of yourself to someone and you didn't even know his name?
LYNN. It was dark.
JAMES. I can't believe this!
LYNN. Shhh!
JAMES. Skip Vanderhooven, of all people …
LYNN. I'm sorry. *(Pause.)*
JAMES. I saved his neck in that class, you know. He never would have passed if it weren't for me.
LYNN. I'm sure you're right.
JAMES. He probably still doesn't know the difference between beryllium and polonium 210.
LYNN. It didn't come up. *(James sulks in silence. Pause. Lynn studies him carefully.)* Do you still want to?
JAMES. Do I sti — of course I still want to marry you.

LYNN. No, I mean ... you know ... tonight?
JAMES. Oh, you mean...?
LYNN. If you think you still can ...
JAMES. What do you mean "if I think I still can"?
LYNN. Well, all this talk about Skip Vanderhooven ...
JAMES. Forget Skip Vanderhooven! Tonight there's just you and me — the only man and woman in the world!
LYNN. Oh, James! *(They kiss passionately for a moment, then James pulls back.)*
JAMES. Wait. Shouldn't we have some kind of ... *(Beat.)*
LYNN. Some kind of what?
JAMES. You know ... protection?
LYNN. Oh, don't you worry, Bunny. I'll protect you ... *(She throws herself on top of him. Blackout.)*

Scene 9

Andrei's apartment. Frank and Mrs. Kravitz have just entered.

FRANK. Anything been touched here?
MRS. KRAVITZ. A hundred times. All by you cops.
FRANK. I'm not a cop. *(Frank starts poking through a rack of LP's.)*
MRS. KRAVITZ. That's right, you're a G-man. White shirt, black shoes, forty-eight stars on your boxer shorts ...
FRANK. Everything his?
MRS. KRAVITZ. Except the furniture and what's on the walls.
FRANK. *The King and I, Carousel ... State Fair*?
MRS. KRAVITZ. He was Russian as a blintz, but he had this thing for Rodgers and Hammerstein. *(Frank pokes through a small trash can.)* Just what are you lookin' for anyway? I thought this fella was the victim.
FRANK. Only as far as the police are concerned. To the FBI, he's a Soviet agent.

MRS. KRAVITZ. No kidding? Soviet agent … I shoulda raised his rent.
FRANK. I'd like to look in the bedroom now. *(They start off, but are interrupted by Andrei, who enters barefoot from the outer door. Seeing them, he begins to duck out again.)* Wait a second wait a second, come back here. *(Andrei returns hesitantly.)* Who are you?
MRS. KRAVITZ. Uh … that's my husband. Nathan Kravitz. CPA. *(Andrei nods in greeting.)*
FRANK. What are you doing in this apartment, Mr. Kravitz? *(Andrei looks to Mrs. Kravitz.)*
MRS. KRAVITZ. Looking for a pair of clean socks, I'll bet. Andrei sometimes borrowed Nate's when his own got wet. Sorry, pet, we're not to remove any hosiery; I'll get you some new at the five-and-dime. *(She starts to usher Andrei out.)*
FRANK. Hold up. How well did you know the deceased?
MRS. KRAVITZ. He can't answer that question.
FRANK. Why not? *(Beat.)*
MRS. KRAVITZ. Because he's mute. *(Beat.)*
FRANK. Mute?
MRS. KRAVITZ. Mute, yes, why, have you never seen a mute? *(Frank considers it.)*
FRANK. I saw a mime once …
MRS. KRAVITZ. Mimes aren't mutes, they're just pretending. Go home, Nate, I'll handle this …
FRANK. Wait a second:
MRS. KRAVITZ. *(Sotto voce.)* Don't you think he's self-conscious enough?
FRANK. How does he communicate with you?
MRS. KRAVITZ. With a complex system of hand gestures, body signals, and facial movements. Right, dear? *(Beat. Andrei, unsure, simply nods.)* See?
FRANK. Ask him something for me.
MRS. KRAVITZ. Ask him yourself, he's not deaf.
FRANK. How well did you know Mr. Borchevsky? *(Pause.)*
MRS. KRAVITZ. Go ahead, Nate, answer the question; I'll translate. *(Andrei looks from one to the other, then begins to gesticulate in a faltering sign language.)*
FRANK. What did he say?

MRS. KRAVITZ. He said because they were about the same size, they sometimes shared clothing, that's all.
FRANK. Huh. Did he ever mention meeting someone from out of town?
MRS. KRAVITZ. I told you, Andrei kept to himself.
FRANK. I'd like your husband's answer, if you don't mind. *(They both look to Andrei, who responds more confidently, more elaborately, more convincingly.)* Well?
MRS. KRAVITZ. He says he once shared a cab with Norman Vincent Peale.
FRANK. Did he ever receive postcards with cryptic messages? *(Andrei goes all out, including foot stomps, forehead slaps, etc. It's long and drawn out. Frank turns to Mrs. Kravitz, very interested.)*
MRS. KRAVITZ. "Greetings from Lake Tahoe." *(Beat. Frank turns back to Andrei, suspiciously.)*
FRANK. What part of that was "Lake Tahoe"? *(Andrei repeats some gesture.)* Uh huh.
MRS. KRAVITZ. If that's all the questions you've got —
FRANK. Just one more thing, Mrs. Kravitz. *(Turning to Andrei.)* Did he ever mention the name Olga Sergeevna?
MRS. KRAVITZ. Sure, it's the name of his boat.
FRANK. I don't mean his boat, I mean his wife — a former Soviet journalist. Joe Stalin sent her to Siberia. We believe your tenant was recruited as a spy to keep her alive. *(To Andrei.)* Did he ever mention Olga Sergeevna? *(Andrei looks at Mrs. Kravitz, then back at Frank. He shakes his head.)*
MRS. KRAVITZ. He says Andrei didn't live in the past. If he did have a wife back home, she might as well not even exist.
FRANK. This *(He shakes his head.)* means all that?
MRS. KRAVITZ. It's like "Aloha," it has many meanings. *(Blackout.)*

Scene 10

In darkness:

ANNOUNCER. *(V.O.)* Welcome to Madison Municipal Airport, your gateway to the Badger State. Will the Shriners from Lansing please remove your tiny motorcycles from the tarmac? *(Lights up on the airport. Lynn stands by James, who carries an army duffel and a paper bag.)* Flight twenty-six for San Francisco now boarding. Now boarding flight number twenty-six …
JAMES. All right, we've only got a few minutes. Where's your mother?
LYNN. She's buying you flight insurance.
JAMES. Then listen carefully: Tomorrow night at ten you'll meet a man named Hermes on the Boston Fish Pier.
LYNN. Is that his first name or his last name?
JAMES. That's his code name. In case we get caught.
LYNN. Oh, James …
JAMES. You'll be traveling as "Jane Smith." I already booked a room for you at the boardinghouse across from the harbor. Now the man will be waiting on Pier 17 under a billboard for kippers. When you get close, just pull out the microfilm. *(He removes a yellow box from the paper bag and hands it to her.)*
LYNN. This is a box of Velveeta.
JAMES. The microfilm's buried inside the cheese.
LYNN. It's not cheese.
JAMES. What?
LYNN. Velveeta's not cheese, it's some kind of weird petroleum product.
JAMES. Whatever it is, the microfilm's inside. Now, there's a secret code that'll let you be sure you've got the right man, and you've got to memorize it.
LYNN. Okay …
JAMES. Repeat after me: You say, "A wonderful bird is the pelican."

LYNN. "A wonderful bird is the pelican."
JAMES. And he says, "His bill will hold more than his belican."
LYNN. "His bill will hold more than his belican." That's not too hard …
JAMES. There's more. You say, "He can take in his beak … "
LYNN. "He can take in his beak … "
JAMES. And then he says, "Food enough for a week … "
LYNN. Okay …
JAMES. And you say, "But I'm damned if I see how the helican."
LYNN. I can't say that.
JAMES. Of course you can.
LYNN. You're asking me to curse.
JAMES. You're willing to commit a capital offense but not to curse?
LYNN. I was taught by nuns.
JAMES. Look, you don't have to say the last line, okay? If the man responds right to the other two, you'll know it's him.
LYNN. Okay.
JAMES. One more thing: if — *(Mrs. McCarthy enters.)*
MRS. McCARTHY. There you are! *(Lynn stuffs the Velveeta box into the paper bag.)* I've been looking everywhere. James, your flight is boarding.
LYNN. He knows, Mother.
MRS. McCARTHY. Well, listen to you! And I just insured your fiancé, for a hundred and fifty dollars.
JAMES. You didn't have to do that, ma'am.
MRS. McCARTHY. Nonsense — you know what you'd have to pay for a good coffin nowadays?
LYNN. Mother, if you don't mind, we're saying goodbye? *(Beat.)*
MRS. McCARTHY. It doesn't seem to matter whether I mind or not. *(She exits. Lynn looks after her.)*
LYNN. She comes from insurance people.
JAMES. All right, now if for some reason you can't get to the pier, or he doesn't show up, the fallback meeting is the following Tuesday, same time, same place.
LYNN. The following Tuesday.
JAMES. Right.
ANNOUNCER. *(V.O.)* Last call for flight number twenty-six, / flight number twenty-six last call for boarding.

LYNN. Oh, Bunny ...
JAMES. I gotta go.
LYNN. You will come back, won't you?
JAMES. Of course I will.
LYNN. And we'll get married? Somehow?
JAMES. I'll talk to the chaplain about it, find out some way we can —
MRS. McCARTHY. *(Reentering.)* James, you're going to miss your plane!
LYNN. Call me?
JAMES. I will. And you call me. *(They kiss desperately. Mrs. McCarthy covers her ears.)*
MRS. McCARTHY. Just pretend I'm not here ... *(When they're done, James exits and Lynn bursts into tears.)* Oh, now, don't you worry. When you're young it always seems like they'll never come back. Then, when you're older you wish they'd stay away longer ... *(Noticing the bag.)* What's that, a parting gift? *(Mrs. McCarthy pulls out the box of Velveeta.)*
LYNN. Uh ...
MRS. McCARTHY. Cheese? Why did he give you cheese? *(She shouts after James.)* WE LIVE IN WISCONSIN! *(Blackout.)*

Scene 11

Split scene, night. On one side of the stage, Maggie's apartment; on the other, Mrs. Kravitz's bedroom. Lights up full on Maggie working at a small kitchen table, a file of papers spread before her. Frank enters with a key.

FRANK. You're workin' late.
MAGGIE. Look who's callin' the kettle black.
FRANK. Hadda make a print of Andrei's shoe to send down to Washington.
MAGGIE. You went to the Kravitz place?

FRANK. First thing this morning. Some piece of work, huh?
MAGGIE. You mean with the wisecracks?
FRANK. Wisecracks?
MAGGIE. Like some joker offa *Dragnet*.
FRANK. I guess I got distracted by all the … *(Exaggerated sign language.)*
MAGGIE. What do you mean?
FRANK. You know, the … *(Even more exaggerated sign language.)*
MAGGIE. What the hell are you doin'?
FRANK. You know, the arms flailin', the feet stompin'…?
MAGGIE. I must've missed it.
FRANK. You'd have to be blind!
MAGGIE. Well you'd have to be deaf to miss all the wisecracks!
FRANK. Wouldn't make a difference, considerin' he's mute! *(Beat.)*
MAGGIE. Who's mute?
FRANK. Mr. Kravitz!
MAGGIE. "Mister"?
FRANK. Of course, who'd you think? *(Beat.)*
MAGGIE. She told me she was divorced.
FRANK. They seemed plenty married to me. *(Lights crossfade to the Kravitz bedroom. Andrei and Mrs. Kravitz in bed.)*
MRS. KRAVITZ. What? *(Andrei sits up.)* I thought you liked that thing with your earlobe. *(Pause. Mrs. Kravitz sits up.)* You want me to sing "Bali H'ai" again? *(Andrei turns away from her.)* Look, if you don't want to, we don't have to. Yesterday you were randy as a goat. *(Pause. Mrs. Kravitz sighs.)* So you want to get up? Watch Dinah Shore? *(Andrei shakes his head. She turns his head to face her.)* Why won't you talk to me?
ANDREI. I am mute.
MRS. KRAVITZ. Oh for Christ's — is that what this is all about? *(He turns away again.)* I thought it was pretty clever on my part.
ANDREI. You, clever, yes! You are not idiot waving arms and stomping feet!
MRS. KRAVITZ. Well what was I supposed to say? You waltzing in with a Fed in the room …
ANDREI. My room!
MRS. KRAVITZ. *Andrei's* room, and / Andrei —

ANDREI. "Andrei is dead," I know. *(Pause. She caresses the back of his neck. Crossfade to Maggie's apartment.)*
FRANK. Oh — here. *(He pulls a passport from his pocket and hands it to her.)*
MAGGIE. What's this — Andrei's?
FRANK. Yours.
MAGGIE. What are you doin' with my passport?
FRANK. Makin' sure you're prepared for Havana.
MAGGIE. I told you I'm not ready to marry …
FRANK. No reason to put off the honeymoon.
MAGGIE. Besides, I'm workin' on a case. *(Beat.)*
FRANK. Yeah, well …
MAGGIE. *(Rifling through her papers.)* Look at this: seventeen separate statements — stevedores, tenants … Everybody says he was a bona fide fisherman.
FRANK. Um …
MAGGIE. Meanwhile, Harry can't even give me a cause of death.
FRANK. Mag:
MAGGIE. Could be "asthma, anaphylactic shock, heart attack" —
FRANK. It's only a case.
MAGGIE. Only a case?
FRANK. You can't solve 'em all.
MAGGIE. I been chasin' this guy almost seven years …
FRANK. Then maybe it's time to let someone else chase him.
MAGGIE. I can't give this to somebody else;
FRANK. You don't have a choice.
MAGGIE. I know this killer like the back — *(Beat.)* What did you say?
FRANK. I said you don't have a choice.
MAGGIE. What are you talkin' about?
FRANK. Your lieutenant called the Bureau this afternoon …
MAGGIE. *(Wary.)* So?
FRANK. We've got a new contact on the force.
MAGGIE. He took me off?
FRANK. I'm sorry, Maggie.
MAGGIE. Son of a bimbo! *(She slams the table and rises, pacing.)*
FRANK. I never woulda found out first, but …
MAGGIE. Goddamn chicken-faced —

FRANK. You were out all afternoon.
MAGGIE. What did he tell you?
FRANK. Petey talked to him.
MAGGIE. *What did he say? (Beat.)*
FRANK. He said he couldn't afford to lose the file again. Whatever that means. *(Long pause.)*
MAGGIE. *(Not looking at him.)* Please tell me he didn't give it to McCloskey. *(Frank is silent.)* Shit. *(She sits heavily. Pause.)*
FRANK. McCloskey's not that bad … *(Beat.)* I mean, he's not you, but —
MAGGIE. *(Turning to him.)* McCloskey couldn't find a murderer in Sing Sing. *(She turns away again.)*
FRANK. You're right. I'm sorry, Mag — it stinks. But look at the bright side … *(Beat.)* Now that you're off the case … *(He picks up her passport from the table. Pause.)*
MAGGIE. *(Not looking at him.)* I can't get married while he's still out there. *(Crossfade. Mrs. Kravitz caressing the back of Andrei's neck.)*
MRS. KRAVITZ. You might as well be Mr. Kravitz, there being a vacancy … His wardrobe's certainly a step up.
ANDREI. You forget I have wife already.
MRS. KRAVITZ. Who you haven't seen in six years.
ANDREI. Still she is my wife.
MRS. KRAVITZ. You don't even know if she's alive.
ANDREI. FBI man knows her!
MRS. KRAVITZ. FBI man thinks this *(She gestures wildly.)* means "Lake Tahoe"!
ANDREI. Nathan said every time I deliver I bring her closer to release.
MRS. KRAVITZ. Oh, "Nathan said," well Nathan cleaned out my bank account and woulda killed us both if I hadn't stopped him. Not the world's most reliable source. *(He gets out of bed and moves away.)* Look, haven't I been a wife to you? I never noticed a wedding ring come between us in the dark.
ANDREI. If it was only question of loving, yes, it is you I love, Mrs. Kravitz —
MRS. KRAVITZ. Florence, please …
ANDREI. … but I have not promised God to look after you until death. When sick, when healthy, money, no money, till death.

MRS. KRAVITZ. So, now you're dead.
ANDREI. No. As you say, Andrei is dead. I am just man whose promise outlives his own name. *(Crossfade.)*
MAGGIE. I need you to get me somethin'.
FRANK. Okay, what?
MAGGIE. *(Finally turning to him.)* Andrei's shoe. *(Beat.)*
FRANK. His shoe?
MAGGIE. Do you still have it?
FRANK. I can get you a copy of the print …
MAGGIE. I don't want the print, I want the shoe.
FRANK. Your boss took you off the case.
MAGGIE. Which is why you're gonna help me moonlight.
FRANK. Maggie …
MAGGIE. Can you get it?
FRANK. You could lose your job!
MAGGIE. I'm gonna lose my killer if I don't move quick. *(Pause.)*
FRANK. Yeah, sure, it's at the office.
MAGGIE. I'll get my coat. *(She exits. Frank looks after her.)*
FRANK. You ever finish reading *Moby Dick*?
MAGGIE. *(O.S.)* Nobody finishes *Moby Dick* — it's a classic.
FRANK. I did. Want to know how it ends?
MAGGIE. *(Reentering with her coat.)* Don't tell me they never peg the whale?
FRANK. Oh, they peg him all right. They peg him good. He just takes the whole damn boat down with him.
MAGGIE. What about the narrator, what's-his-name?
FRANK. Ishmael?
MAGGIE. He musta made it.
FRANK. He's the only one. *(He watches her as she finishes putting her coat on.)* All I'm sayin' is watch your back. I don't want you goin' down with the whale. *(She kisses him.)*
MAGGIE. Call me Ishmael. *(She starts out as he looks after her, then he follows. Crossfade.)*
MRS. KRAVITZ. There's a meeting tomorrow. *(He turns.)*
ANDREI. Meeting?
MRS. KRAVITZ. Ten o'clock. Under the billboard.
ANDREI. He told you this?
MRS. KRAVITZ. He never told me anything. But I got eyes and

ears, don't I?
ANDREI. With Hermes dead, there is no meeting.
MRS. KRAVITZ. So you be Hermes. *(Beat.)*
ANDREI. Me?
MRS. KRAVITZ. What's the Los Alamos mole gonna say? Tell him the other Hermes went on a long vacation. Then you deliver the goods at sea, like always.
ANDREI. But Andrei is dead.
MRS. KRAVITZ. The Reds don't know that. We'll keep the cash ourselves this time, head to my sister's place in Guantánamo. Find our own special island … *(She approaches him from behind. Pause.)*
ANDREI. And Olga?
MRS. KRAVITZ. Where is Olga? Show me Olga. Olga's a name on a piece of paper five thousand miles away. *(She stands close behind him.)* Can a piece of paper keep you warm on a cold night? *(She touches him.)* Can it? *(Andrei turns to look at her. Blackout.)*

Scene 12

Music fades as lights come up on the morgue, where Maggie has just handed Harry an election button. The corpse lies on a gurney, as before.

HARRY. For me?
MAGGIE. If you don't already have it.
HARRY. Heck no — I been lookin' for weeks! *(Reading it.)* "Ike and Dick, Sure to Click" …
MAGGIE. Try it on.
HARRY. *(Pinning it on.)* Didn't think you liked Ike.
MAGGIE. Oh, sure: I like Ike, I love Lucy … I'm just wild about Harry.
HARRY. How do I look?
MAGGIE. Like you're ready for the polls. Say, any match on the prints from Washington?

HARRY. Not till tomorrow, maybe Sunday. *(Maggie begins to lift the cloth, but Harry puts his hand on the body.)* Where's McCloskey?
MAGGIE. McCloskey?
HARRY. They said he was takin' over.
MAGGIE. He is, I'm just tyin' up loose ends. Can I have a look? *(Beat. Harry studies her for a moment.)* If you need me to call the Lieutenant …
HARRY. No, go ahead. *(He lets go of the cloth; she lifts it to look at the corpse's face.)* You're lucky we still got him. Normally he'd be broiled by now. No family to claim the body. *(He notices Maggie staring at the body.)* What.
MAGGIE. Something different about this guy.
HARRY. It's the five o'clock shadow. Beard keeps growin' after death.
MAGGIE. No, I mean he … looks familiar.
HARRY. Occupational hazard. The faces all start to look the same. *(Maggie covers the corpse's face again.)* Last week, I coulda sworn a 240-pound dockworker was my mother-in-law. *(Maggie removes a man's shoe from her trenchcoat pocket.)* What's that?
MAGGIE. Mind if I try it on?
HARRY. Shouldn't you have done that in the store? *(Beat.)*
MAGGIE. Let me rephrase the question.
HARRY. Go ahead. I doubt he'll object. *(Harry lifts the cloth to expose the corpse's feet. As Maggie struggles to make it fit, he admires the new button on his coat.)* Y'know, I wasn't too hot on Nixon till he did that Checkers speech on TV. Takes a big man to come on right after Uncle Miltie and cry about his dog. Whoa. *(The shoe is way too small.)*
MAGGIE. Got a shoehorn?
HARRY. What do you make of that?
MAGGIE. Either the feet keep growin' after death … or this guy had worse luck with shoes than me … *(Blackout.)*

Scene 13

City Hall. Frank stands before a counter, above or in front of which is a big sign that reads "Marriage Licenses." Seeing no one, he rings a bell on the counter, then turns away, looking around and tapping his fingers on the counter. In a moment, a dour clerk enters. Frank turns.

FRANK. Oh, hi —
CLERK. Don't tell me you're here for a marriage license. *(Frank looks at the sign.)*
FRANK. Uhhh …
CLERK. Do you have any idea how many marriages end in divorce? *(Beat.)*
FRANK. Well —
CLERK. Nineteen percent.
FRANK. Huh.
CLERK. Russian roulette gives you better odds. *(Beat.)*
FRANK. Is this part of your job?
CLERK. Adlai Stevenson's divorced.
FRANK. I know.
CLERK. Elizabeth Taylor's been married twice, and I wouldn't be surprised if she marries again.
FRANK. Well, I didn't come here to marry Liz Taylor.
CLERK. Even I got divorced, if you can believe that. *(Beat.)*
FRANK. I can't imagine why.
CLERK. My husband left me for a cheap, red-hair-from-a-bottle tart, the creep.
FRANK. *(Looking past her.)* Is the other girl here? I talked with her Tuesday …
CLERK. Men and redheads, I can't understand it.
FRANK. *(Calling past her.)* Hello?
CLERK. I went red for a month in '46, you'd think I was wearin' a see-through blouse.

FRANK. I only came in to pick up my license. I wasn't expecting a lecture on divorce. *(Beat.)*
CLERK. Don't say I didn't warn you … *(She opens a file drawer.)* What's your name?
FRANK. Frank Keller. K-E-L-L —
CLERK. "Abbott, Abernathy, Ackerman, Adams, Aiken, Albertson, Alexander, Allen, Amery, Anderson, Anderson, Anderson" —
FRANK. Maybe you could just skip to the K's…? *(Clerk just looks at Frank, then skips ahead.)*
CLERK. "Kane, Kapp, Kaufman, Kean, Keating, Keith, Keneally, Kidder" —
FRANK. You must have missed me. *(Clerk looks up again.)* Keller: K-E-L —
CLERK. Are you questioning my ability to alphabetize?
FRANK. No …
CLERK. I was hired for my alphabetizational skills.
FRANK. I just want my license.
CLERK. *(Checking another file.)* Are you sure it was supposed to be ready?
FRANK. The girl said Friday …
CLERK. Perhaps an item was missing from your folder …
FRANK. I turned in the passports, paid in cash —
CLERK. *(Removing two paper-clipped pages.)* Oh!
FRANK. Is that it?
CLERK. *(Looking at the second sheet.)* Oh boy …
FRANK. Let me see … *(He reaches for the pages, but Clerk backs up.)*
CLERK. *(Calling off.)* Mr. Gilhooley!
FRANK. What's wrong?
CLERK. *(Calling off.)* I got a 26-B!
FRANK. "26-B"? What's the matter?
CLERK. I'm sorry, I can't give you the license.
FRANK. The girl said three days …
CLERK. Normally yes, but —
FRANK. But nothin' — I filled out the paperwork …
CLERK. Your file's complete, it's just —
FRANK. Just what?

CLERK. I can't permit you to marry this woman.
FRANK. Well why the hell not? *(She turns the marriage license to face him.)*
CLERK. She's already married. *(Blackout.)*

Scene 14

A bridal shop. Late afternoon. A mannequin displays a frilly white number. Mrs. Van Nostrand, the proprietor, enters from offstage speaking to an unseen customer:

MRS. VAN NOSTRAND. Trust me, you'll look so fetching, you may leave the altar with two or three husbands. *(As Mrs. Van Nostrand returns to her work, Maggie enters, looking about her, a bit disoriented. Mrs. Van Nostrand notices her.)* If you're shopping for a Halloween costume, they're across the street.
MAGGIE. Come again?
MRS. VAN NOSTRAND. I'm sorry, are you here for a wedding gown?
MAGGIE. Um, well, I saw your window, and —
MRS. VAN NOSTRAND. *(Crossing to welcome her.)* Please excuse me. You looked so like a fish out of water … Will your mother be joining us?
MAGGIE. She's deceased.
MRS. VAN NOSTRAND. Excellent. Fewer intrusions. Let me see the ring …
MAGGIE. I didn't get one. *(Beat.)*
MRS. VAN NOSTRAND. Then how do you know you're engaged?
MAGGIE. I'm not. *(Pause.)*
MRS. VAN NOSTRAND. My dear: I can sell you the dress and accessories, but you'll have to provide the groom yourself.
MAGGIE. I mean, he proposed, I just … I'm sorry, you're right, I don't belong here …

MRS. VAN NOSTRAND. Nonsense.
MAGGIE. I'll come back when I have more time …
MRS. VAN NOSTRAND. My dear, if you're as old as I think, you haven't got time to waste. *(Escorting her into the store.)* Would you like some tea?
MAGGIE. Don't go to any trouble.
MRS. VAN NOSTRAND. No trouble at all. *(She rings a small bell.)* I keep my latest husband on hand for just such occasions. *(Herbert shuffles in obediently.)*
HERBERT. Yes, dear?
MRS. VAN NOSTRAND. We'll need some tea and shortbread.
HERBERT. Yes, dear. *(He exits.)*
MRS. VAN NOSTRAND. Oh … *(She rings the bell again. He reenters.)*
HERBERT. Yes, dear?
MRS. VAN NOSTRAND. And bring some schnapps.
HERBERT. Yes, dear. *(He exits.)*
MRS. VAN NOSTRAND. It's wonderful how you can train them with a bell … *(She rings the bell again. He reenters.)*
HERBERT. Yes, dear?
MRS. VAN NOSTRAND. Nothing.
HERBERT. Yes, dear. *(He exits.)*
MRS. VAN NOSTRAND. Now: What sort of a man is your intended? Other than cheap, I mean.
MAGGIE. Well, he's … very persistent.
MRS. VAN NOSTRAND. Go on.
MAGGIE. Can't stomach small talk, doesn't like dinner parties … hates a Hollywood happy ending …
MRS. VAN NOSTRAND. Sounds as sentimental as a cactus.
MAGGIE. He might seem that way to some people. But he also has a soft part. Just takes a while to find it.
MRS. VAN NOSTRAND. My husband has a soft part, too. *(Regretfully, looking off.)* Didn't take long to find.
MAGGIE. *(Checking her watch.)* I should go …
MRS. VAN NOSTRAND. Don't be silly.
MAGGIE. I'm meeting him for dinner next door …
MRS. VAN NOSTRAND. If he's persistent he won't mind waiting … Come, I'll show you the collection. *(As she leads Maggie offstage,*

she calls to the dressing area:) Still conscious in there?
LYNN. *(O.S.)* I'm just coming out.
MRS. VAN NOSTRAND. The mirrors are quivering in anticipation. *(She opens a door or curtain.)* There you go …
MAGGIE. *(Exiting.)* Oh my …
MRS. VAN NOSTRAND. A winter wonderland. *(Lynn enters from the dressing room, looking absolutely perfect in a stunning white dress.)* Try on anything that quickens your pulse. Don't peek at the price tag! *(Mrs. Van Nostrand turns around and gasps in delight.)* Lovely! Absolutely splendid!
LYNN. Do you think?
MRS. VAN NOSTRAND. Here, have a look in the three-way. *(They go to the downstage "mirrors.")* Oh, yes, very nice … The perfect gown for a first wedding. *(Mrs. Van Nostrand adjusts the dress as Lynn studies herself.)*
LYNN. You make it sound like I should have more than one.
MRS. VAN NOSTRAND. Well, "if at first you don't succeed" … One marriage fails, but the heart still flutters; a second falters, but the loins still yearn.
LYNN. Why wouldn't we succeed?
MRS. VAN NOSTRAND. No reason, dear; no reason at all. But should the glimmer fade, you'll know where to find me the next time around. Will the groom be wearing his dress uniform?
LYNN. Dress uniform?
MRS. VAN NOSTRAND. You said he's stationed in the South Pacific.
LYNN. Oh, he's not a soldier, he's a scientist. They just made him enlist because he's doing some covert work for the army. *Secret —* I meant secret work. In the good sense. You know, nothing … furtive. *(Mrs. Van Nostrand nods vaguely and continues adjusting Lynn's dress. Maggie enters adjusting a poofy white dress above her clunky regulation shoes.)*
MRS. VAN NOSTRAND. *(Seeing Maggie.)* Well, now, aren't you a vision in white.
MAGGIE. I feel like the Good Witch of the North.
MRS. KRAVITZ. Nonsense, Glinda was pink. *(To Lynn.)* I have the perfect veil for this. Let me see if I can find it. *(She exits. Lynn examines herself in the "mirrors" as Maggie watches for a moment.)*

MAGGIE. You belong on top of a wedding cake.
LYNN. Excuse me?
MAGGIE. That's a compliment. You look like half of the perfect ornament. *(Beat.)*
LYNN. I wish I knew for sure …
MAGGIE. *(Gesturing to the mirror.)* Don't take my word for it.
LYNN. Not that; I mean I wish I knew — never mind. *(She returns to the mirrors. Pause.)*
MAGGIE. We all have doubts.
LYNN. Not like mine.
MAGGIE. Does he love you?
LYNN. He says he does.
MAGGIE. Seems to have put his money where his mouth is.
LYNN. Oh. Yeah.
MAGGIE. Then what's the problem? *(Beat.)*
LYNN. I'm carrying another man's baby. *(Pause.)*
MAGGIE. Oh! *(Mrs. Van Nostrand enters with an elaborate veil.)*
MRS. VAN NOSTRAND. Here we are: headdress for a queen!
LYNN. Oh my …
MRS. VAN NOSTRAND. Simply the cherry on the sundae. Hold still … *(Mrs. Van Nostrand arranges the veil on Lynn's head as Maggie considers herself in the "mirrors," stepping back to look at the dress from all sides. Frank enters, carrying a flask. He regards Maggie for a moment before speaking.)*
FRANK. You got a lotta gall wearin' white.
MAGGIE. Frank! *(She turns.)*
FRANK. Wouldn't a red letter A suit you better? *(He takes a drink from the flask.)*
MRS. VAN NOSTRAND. Can I help you?
FRANK. Thanks, I can drink this by myself.
MAGGIE. What's wrong?
FRANK. Oh, nothin' …
MRS. VAN NOSTRAND. Unless you're shopping for —
FRANK. I just paid a visit to City Hall where I ran across an interesting piece of paper. *(He removes it and looks at it.)*
MAGGIE. What were you doing at City Hall?
FRANK. Hopin' to pick up one of these. *(He holds the marriage license in front of him.)* Trouble is, the name next to yours wasn't

mine. And here you are tryin' on a wedding dress.
MAGGIE. Frank ...
FRANK. As an officer, I thought you'd know that havin' two husbands was against the law. *(Herbert enters with tea, shortbread, and schnapps on a tray.)*
MRS. VAN NOSTRAND. Herbert:
HERBERT. Yes, dear? *(He sets it down.)*
MRS. VAN NOSTRAND. Eject this ruffian immediately.
HERBERT. Yes, dear. *(He moves toward Frank.)*
FRANK. Get your henpecked hands offa me! *(Frank punches Herbert in the stomach, sending him to the floor.)*
MAGGIE. Frank!
MRS. VAN NOSTRAND. How dare you strike a spineless man! I'm calling the police ...
MAGGIE. I am the police.
MRS. VAN NOSTRAND. Well, that was fast.
FRANK. You want to explain this?
MAGGIE. Of course I want —
FRANK. Then explain it.
MAGGIE. I will; just let —
FRANK. Explain it now.
MAGGIE. Frank, don't make a fool of yourself.
FRANK. Oh, you already took care of that, Mrs. Murphy. Picture me strollin' into City Hall like a man with a winnin' lottery ticket. Picture me sidlin' up to the counter to pick up a brand-new marriage license ...
MAGGIE. I give you my word —
FRANK. Your word's worth less than a piss in the harbor! *(Enraged, he shreds the marriage license. Then:)* How could you?
MAGGIE. When you hear the whole story —
FRANK. How could you? *(Beat.)*
MAGGIE. I ... I'm sorry. *(Pause. Frank chuckles ironically and shakes his head.)*
FRANK. How am I gonna face the rest of my life? *(He turns and starts out. Mrs. Van Nostrand takes a parting shot:)*
MRS. VAN NOSTRAND. You still should have gotten her a ring! *(Frank stops and turns.)*
FRANK. I got just one thing to say to you, lady. *(He pulls out a*

pistol from a shoulder holster. Lynn and Mrs. Van Nostrand scream, Herbert cowers.)
MAGGIE. No, Frank! *(Frank deftly turns and shoots the mannequin, which topples over. Then he walks to the mannequin, straddles it, and empties the pistol into it. He reholsters the gun.)*
LYNN. I think I'm going to be sick … *(Frank exits.)*
MAGGIE. Wait! *(She rushes to the door.)*
LYNN. I am, I'm going to be sick! *(She runs off. Silence. Mrs. Van Nostrand picks up a glass of schnapps and considers the wreckage before her.)*
MRS. VAN NOSTRAND. Well! Now you know why it's bad luck for the groom to see the bride before the wedding! *(She downs the schnapps. Blackout.)*

End Act One

ACT TWO

Scene 15

Lights up on one side of the stage, where Lynn stands holding a telephone; on the other, a telephone receiver hangs down from a "wall." After a moment, James enters sleepily in his underwear and picks up the phone.

JAMES. Hello? *(Pause.)* Hello?
LYNN. James? *(Pause.)* Hello?
JAMES. Lynn?
LYNN. It's me, Lynn.
JAMES. Can you hear me?
LYNN. Didn't they tell you?
JAMES. I know, / are you okay?
LYNN. I can hear you loud and clear, there just seems to be some weird delay or / something — what?
JAMES. All they said was I had a call, they didn't / tell me —
LYNN. I'm fine.
JAMES. What? Oh —
LYNN. I just / wanted to talk to you.
JAMES. I guess the operator didn't warn you, this overseas line has some weird delay …
LYNN. You said to call around dinnertime, / so I — what?
JAMES. Everything's okay, then?
LYNN. I'm hearing that too.
JAMES. Dinnertime?
LYNN. It's awful. No, everything's fine.
JAMES. It's two in the morn — what?
LYNN. Didn't you say dinnertime?
JAMES. Maybe we should / take turns talking.

LYNN. Maybe we should alternate, you know, / take turns.
JAMES. Okay. You start.
LYNN. What? *(Beat.)* Yeah, let's do that. You start. *(Beat.)* You want me to / start?
JAMES. Okay, I'll start. How was your trip to Boston? Did you find the / boardinghouse?
LYNN. Now I'm confused.
JAMES. What — no, I said I'll start. / *Stop talking.*
LYNN. It was fine, I'm calling from the boardinghouse now — oh. Okay. *(Beat.)*
JAMES. Do you miss me? *(Beat.)* I'll wait till you respond. *(Beat.)*
LYNN. Oh, you bet I — oops. You bet I do. Do you miss me? *(Beat.)* I'm done. *(Pause.)*
JAMES. Only like crazy. *(Beat.)* Over. *(Pause.)*
LYNN. Is it my turn now? *(Beat.)* What do you mean "over"? *(Beat.)*
JAMES. Yes, it's your — what? *(Beat.)* It means you're done talking. *(Beat.)* Over.
LYNN. I went to a bridal shop today … oh, "over," like pilots, I get it … Over.
JAMES. Did you try on a dress? Yeah, just like pilots. *(Beat.)*
LYNN. I did, but …
JAMES. Over.
LYNN. … something happened.
JAMES. Hey, guess what? One of the guys here is actually Quaker, can you believe it? What happened? *(Beat.)*
LYNN. Really? Over. *(Beat.)* Oh, / nothing, just — oops.
JAMES. Yeah, he told me all about getting married to his wife in a Quaker wedding, and it sounded so … well, pretty. Over. *(Long pause.)*
LYNN. Do you still want to go through with this thing? *(Beat.)* Over. *(Beat.)*
JAMES. Of course I do! Don't you? Over. *(Pause.)*
LYNN. I'm only doing it because it means so much to you. *(Pause.)*
JAMES. You are? You seemed so excited when I gave you the ring. *(Beat.)*
LYNN. Of course. But it goes against — oh! *(Beat.)* *Oh* …
JAMES. What do you mean? Don't you want to get married?

LYNN. You think I mean getting married … *(Beat.)*
JAMES. Unless you mean the meet — *(Sotto voce.)* you mean the meeting on the fish pier? *(Beat.)* Over?
LYNN. *(Realizing it herself.)* Well, maybe, I … I don't know … *(Pause.)*
JAMES. You do mean the meeting, right? Over. *(Pause.)*
LYNN. I'm not sure. Over. *(Beat.)* I better go. *(Beat.)*
JAMES. Not sure about what? *(Pause.)*
LYNN. If I do the one whether I can do the other. *(Mrs. Kravitz enters with laundry.)*
MRS. KRAVITZ. Wrap it up, Missy.
LYNN. Yes, Mrs. Kravitz. *(Mrs. Kravitz exits.)*
JAMES. What do you mean if you do the one…?
LYNN. We'll talk.
JAMES. Did you just call me Missy?
LYNN. Good night. Morning, whatever.
JAMES. When? *(Beat.)*
LYNN. I miss you.
JAMES. Lynn? *(Beat.)* We'll talk when?
LYNN. Over.
JAMES. I miss you, too. Over. *(Beat. Lynn hangs up.)* I love you. *(Beat. Lynn bursts into tears.)* Over. *(Pause.)* Did you hear me? *(Pause.)* Lynn? *(Pause. James hangs up.)* Over.

Scene 16

An off-the-beaten-path saloon. Andrei sits at the bar alone. In front of him are half a dozen empty shot glasses. He holds a full glass in one hand, a teaspoon in the other, and carefully pours the contents of the shot glass into the teaspoon. Then he sets the glass on the table, raises the spoon in a silent toast, and slurps the contents down.

Maggie enters as Andrei refills his spoon, sets down the glass, repeats the toast, and downs it. She looks around for a moment, then crosses to the bar as Andrei finishes pouring a third spoonful.

MAGGIE. Excuse me … *(Andrei throws his hand up.)*
ANDREI. Don't talk or I spill.
MAGGIE. Okay … *(Andrei drinks, lowers his arm, and looks at her.)* Sorry to bother you. I came here looking for someone.
ANDREI. You and everybody else. *(He pours.)*
MAGGIE. Someone in particular. My fiancé. About this tall? Buzz cut, dark blue suit?
ANDREI. Good-looking man?
MAGGIE. Yes!
ANDREI. Square jaw, broad shoulder?
MAGGIE. Yes, have you seen him?
ANDREI. No.
MAGGIE. Oh.
ANDREI. But, if he is your fiancé, you must believe he is good-looking, square-jaw, broad-shoulder, yes?
MAGGIE. I was hoping to find him here. *(She slides onto the bar stool next to him.)*
ANDREI. Why here?
MAGGIE. Because he gave up drinking. *(Beat.)*
ANDREI. You were hoping he will start again?

MAGGIE. No, I know he's started again; I was hoping he wasn't out drinking alone ...
ANDREI. Ah. You are having lovers' fight. Throwing, breaking, names being yelled at ...
MAGGIE. You seem to know a lot about lovers' fights.
ANDREI. *(Shrugging.)* I am married man. *(He pours another spoonful as Maggie watches.)*
MAGGIE. Can I ask you a personal — *(Andrei holds up his hand in warning.)* Sorry. *(Andrei drinks from the spoon.)*
ANDREI. Now you can ask your personal.
MAGGIE. Why are you drinking vodka from a spoon?
ANDREI. When I use fork, it spills in my lap. *(Beat.)*
MAGGIE. Let me rephrase the question:
ANDREI. With spoon I don't drink too much. Bar man! *(Maggie surveys the empty shot glasses.)*
MAGGIE. It doesn't seem to have slowed you down ...
ANDREI. You should see when I don't use spoon. *(A young bartender enters.)*
BARTENDER. Yeah?
ANDREI. One more glass.
BARTENDER. You said this was your last.
ANDREI. I am ordering for lady.
MAGGIE. Oh, that's all right ...
ANDREI. And extra spoon.
MAGGIE. Really, I'm fine.
ANDREI. You don't want to use my spoon; I have a cold. *(Maggie smiles and relents:)*
MAGGIE. Okay. *(The Bartender exits. Andrei drinks another spoonful as Maggie watches. Then:)* Where are you from? *(Andrei looks at her.)*
ANDREI. Why?
MAGGIE. I ... thought I heard an accent, that's all.
ANDREI. Oklahoma.
MAGGIE. Really?
ANDREI. Where the wind comes sweeping down the plain.
MAGGIE. It didn't sound like an Oklahoma accent.
ANDREI. Everybody tells me this. How many Oklahoma people do you know?

MAGGIE. None.
ANDREI. One.
MAGGIE. One? *(She realizes what he means.)* One. *(They smile.)* You're a long way from Oklahoma.
ANDREI. You too.
MAGGIE. What part are you from?
ANDREI. The coast. *(Beat.)*
MAGGIE. Okay … *(The Bartender arrives with a full shot glass.)*
BARTENDER. *(To Andrei.)* After this it's Shirley Temples. *(He sets it down in front of Maggie and turns to go.)*
ANDREI. And spoon? *(Bartender stops, removes the spoon from his shirt pocket, and sets it down.)*
BARTENDER. Let me know if he gets fresh, Miss. *(He exits.)*
ANDREI. Would you like to toast?
MAGGIE. Are you getting fresh?
ANDREI. At this hour, no one is fresh. *(He raises his spoon. She pours from her shot glass into his spoon, then into hers.)*
MAGGIE. Well?
ANDREI. Lady first.
MAGGIE. "Wet the whistle, warm the heart." *(They drink.)* So, is your wife wanderin' about tonight lookin' for you?
ANDREI. Oh, no. We are strange. *(Beat.)*
MAGGIE. Strange?
ANDREI. Yes.
MAGGIE. What do you mean you're strange?
ANDREI. No longer do we live together.
MAGGIE. I don't under — Oh, you're estranged …
ANDREI. Yes.
MAGGIE. I'm sorry.
ANDREI. Yes. We are strange many years. *(Pause.)* I have betrayed her.
MAGGIE. Oh.
ANDREI. I am betraying her now. *(Andrei checks his watch.)* At this very moment, I am betraying her.
MAGGIE. We're only talkin' …
ANDREI. Not the talking.
MAGGIE. And drinking liquor from … little spoons …
ANDREI. Not the little spoons.

MAGGIE. *(Indicating the empty glasses in front of him.)* Well, unless she owns the bar across the street —
ANDREI. You have seen boardbill?
MAGGIE. "Boardbill"?
ANDREI. Ogilby's. "Put the fish into your pocket" …
MAGGIE. You mean "billboard"?
ANDREI. Yes, of course I mean. What is "boardbill"? Nothing. Silliness. You see this billboard?
MAGGIE. Sure, what about it?
ANDREI. It is portrait of marriage.
MAGGIE. Actually, it's an advertisement for kippers …
ANDREI. What do you see?
MAGGIE. On the billboard?
ANDREI. Yes, in advertisement, what do you see? *(As Maggie pictures it, the onstage billboard glows faintly.)*
MAGGIE. Well … two fishermen in a dory pulling —
ANDREI. Not two fishermen.
MAGGIE. There might be ships in the background, but —
ANDREI. Not two fishermen.
MAGGIE. All right, how many do you see?
ANDREI. One.
MAGGIE. One?
ANDREI. One fisherman. And his wife.
MAGGIE. His wife.
ANDREI. It is portrait of marriage.
MAGGIE. What makes you think that's his wife?
ANDREI. This is famous American painting! You think famous American painter paint this for selling the kippers? No! Famous painter knows that marriage is a little dory.
MAGGIE. A little dory.
ANDREI. A little dory with a little leak.
MAGGIE. I'll take your word for it.
ANDREI. Yes, please take my word, young bride-to-be. And any good boat can take a little leak if always somebody bails it out. BUT: If you ignore this leak, you both drown. It is simple as this. If you see leak, and both say, "Let other one bail," you drown. Even if you cram your nets with fish, till bursting almost, if no one bails, you only sink your little boat faster.

MAGGIE. What if your marriage doesn't have a little leak?
ANDREI. All marriage have leak.
MAGGIE. What if it doesn't?
ANDREI. Then you are ignoring, and you will drown. *(Maggie considers this. Pause.)* He has betrayed you, Mr. Broad Shoulder?
MAGGIE. No; I can't imagine it.
ANDREI. Then you have betrayed him. *(Beat.)*
MAGGIE. I certainly never meant to. *(Andrei nods.)*
ANDREI. You and everybody else.
MAGGIE. Somebody betrayed me first. A long time ago. *(Beat.)*
ANDREI. Yes? *(Beat.)*
MAGGIE. Yes what.
ANDREI. Yes, and…?
MAGGIE. That's it, end of story.
ANDREI. No, no, not end; *(He sets down his spoon.)* beginning of story. *(He settles in for the story.)*
MAGGIE. One teaspoon of vodka and you expect me to bare my soul to a perfect stranger?
ANDREI. Of course not. Forgive me. *(Beat. He slides Maggie's shot glass towards her.)*
MAGGIE. That's more like it. *(She drinks it in one shot, placing the glass back on the table. Pause.)*
ANDREI. Well?
MAGGIE. I almost killed him once. *(Beat.)*
ANDREI. Mr. Broad Shoulder?
MAGGIE. My husband, before him. Week after we took our vows.
ANDREI. Talk about "honeymoon is over" …
MAGGIE. I made deviled scrod, my mom's old standby. Measured everything twice, terrified of blowing it. Set the table fancy … I make him shut his eyes, lead him to the table, even put the fork in his hand. He takes one bite. Smiles. Takes another. And starts to gag. I mean bug-eyed, blue in the face. I'm sure I screwed up the recipe — not enough butter, too much tabasco…? Turns out he's allergic to fish. If you can imagine such a thing. So I drag him out to the Dodge, throw him in the back, and run a dozen red lights on the way to the hospital, prayin' like a nun. Doctor said if we got there two minutes later … *(She shakes her head,*

recalling it.) If I knew then what I know now … I would have stopped at every light. *(Beat.)*
ANDREI. This man hurt you deeply. *(Beat. She checks her watch.)*
MAGGIE. Listen, I ought to get going …
ANDREI. Not so soon?
MAGGIE. Too much chitchat.
ANDREI. One spoon for the road…? *(Beat.)*
MAGGIE. All right. *(Andrei pours one for Maggie, then empties his glass into his own spoon.)* Your turn.
ANDREI. *Na zdorov'e.* (*He drinks. Maggie regards him for a moment, then drinks.)*
MAGGIE. What did you say?
ANDREI. "For health." *(Maggie places her spoon on the bar.)*
MAGGIE. Did you by any chance know Andrei Borchevsky? *(Pause.)*
ANDREI. Yes, I know him.
MAGGIE. Did you know he was found dead a few days ago?
ANDREI. I have heard this. It is very sad.
MAGGIE. You were friends, then?
ANDREI. I cannot say I knew him well. But I regret very much he is dead.
MAGGIE. If you hear anything that might help me find his killer, would you let me know? *(She hands him her card. He reads it. Beat.)*
ANDREI. Of course.
MAGGIE. I appreciate it. *(Maggie starts to leave.)*
ANDREI. Good luck also finding Mr. Broad Shoulder.
MAGGIE. *(Turning back.)* Thanks. *(She starts out again.)*
ANDREI. And when you do … *(She turns back again.)*
MAGGIE. Yeah?
ANDREI. *(Demonstrating with his spoon.)* Don't forget to bail. *(Blackout.)*

Scene 17

The fish pier. Night. Frank sits on the dock fishing; a bait bucket and fishing gear sit nearby. Occasionally, he takes a swig from a flask. Lynn enters tentatively, wearing sunglasses and carrying a handbag. She inconspicuously tries to get a better look at Frank, then checks her watch and looks around for anyone else who might be nearby. Finally, she reaches into her handbag and removes the box of Velveeta, placing it on a wooden pile. Frank notices, takes another swig, then addresses her:

FRANK. Brought the secret weapon, huh? *(Beat.)*
LYNN. Excuse me?
FRANK. The cheese. Fish can't resist it.
LYNN. Oh.
FRANK. Like lambs to the slaughter. All else fails, break out the Velveeta. *(Lynn smiles pleasantly but, unsure of Frank's identity, removes the Velveeta from the pile and holds it in her arms instead.)* Course, it's customary to dangle it in the water. They usually won't crawl up to unwrap it.
LYNN. I … didn't really come here to fish.
FRANK. Just as well. Seems the only thing bitin' here lately is dead guys. *(Beat.)*
LYNN. Excuse me?
FRANK. No, excuse me. I'm a little harder-boiled than usual tonight. *(Pause. Lynn looks at Frank more closely.)*
LYNN. The dress shop …
FRANK. Huh?
LYNN. This afternoon …
FRANK. Oh God … *(He leans his head on a railing or pile.)*
LYNN. I'm sorry — I shouldn't have recognized you … *(She tries to see his face.)* Are you all right?
FRANK. *(Snapping back.)* Oh yeah; I'm fine.

LYNN. I didn't mean to make you feel worse.
FRANK. I can't imagine how you could. *(He takes a swig.)* Nice rock.
LYNN. Oh — thank you.
FRANK. Inscribed?
LYNN. Uh huh.
FRANK. Let me see it. *(Beat.)*
LYNN. Well ...
FRANK. Never mind. I know I must not look very reputable ... *(He turns away.)*
LYNN. No, it's okay. *(She removes the ring and hands it to him.)*
FRANK. *(Reading.)* "One plus one equals ... " *(He turns the ring sideways.)* Eight.
LYNN. Infinity.
FRANK. This says "eight."
LYNN. That's an infinity symbol. Because our love was infinite.
FRANK. "Was"?
LYNN. Is! Is, Was, Will Be ... *(She snatches the ring back.)* That's what infinite means. *(She pops the ring into her pocket. Frank regards her dubiously.)*
FRANK. Uh huh. *(He turns away again. Pause.)* I proposed with a ring the first time. Inscribed.
LYNN. The first time?
FRANK. She was older than me — Christ, I was just a kid — and she seemed so ... worldly, so sophisticated. Taught me how to drink. Initiated me into the ... mysteries of the bedroom. I'd never even seen a brassiere before — I'm sorry, does this embarrass you?
LYNN. No.
FRANK. I mean a brassiere you could touch and take off, slip it down the shoulders ... like that. Feeling skin so smooth and soft, and having soft, smooth skin to feel it with ... *(He looks out, lost in the memory. Pause.)*
LYNN. What was her name?
FRANK. Hmm? Oh — Ethel. Ethel Mirman. *(Beat.)*
LYNN. Ethel Merman?
FRANK. I called her Pinky.
LYNN. The Ethel Merman, the one who sang / "There's —
FRANK. "There's No Business Like Show Business"?

LYNN. Yeah!
FRANK. No; different Ethel Mirman.
LYNN. Oh.
FRANK. This one packaged fish for Ogilby's.
LYNN. Well … did you ever get married?
FRANK. The week after I proposed, I found Pinky in the bedroom with another young man.
LYNN. Oh no …
FRANK. It's not what you think; they were both fully dressed. She was just givin' him the ring to hock. *(He turns back to look at her.)* He was her son. From a "previous engagement." *(He looks out again.)*
LYNN. I am so sorry …
FRANK. It was a long time ago.
LYNN. I mean about today. *(Beat.)*
FRANK. Yeah. Well. My skin's not so soft anymore. Though I never thought I'd be fooled again — being in the business of secrets and lies. *(Lynn sees Frank in a new light. She gathers her courage, clears her throat, and makes a leap of faith:)*
LYNN. "A wonderful bird is the pelican … "
FRANK. *(Beat. Frank turns back to her.)* Huh?
LYNN. I said, "A wonderful bird is the pelican … "
FRANK. Ogden Nash, right?
LYNN. What?
FRANK. "His bill will hold more than his belican"?
LYNN. "He can take in his beak … "
FRANK. "Food enough for a week … "
LYNN. But I'm darned if I see how the heck he can! *(Frank is a little baffled by the final line, but Lynn is relieved and euphoric:)* Oh, thank goodness! I was hoping it was you …
FRANK. Hopin'…?
LYNN. Well, you were the only one out here, but you sure don't look like what I imagined. More like a … G-man or something! Anyway, here you go. *(She thrusts the Velveeta box into his hands.)*
FRANK. Oh. Thanks.
LYNN. The thing's inside the cheese.
FRANK. Thing?
LYNN. You know, the "microfilm." Actually, it's not real cheese.

It's some kind of weird petroleum — *(Beat.)* Oh my God … *(She snatches the box back.)*
FRANK. *(Catching on.)* Hey.
LYNN. Oh my God!
FRANK. Wait … *(But Lynn turns and runs like hell, yelling:)*
LYNN. Ohmygodohmygodohmygodohmygodohmygod…! *(Frank starts after her, but gets entangled in his fishing gear and bait bucket.)*
FRANK. Stop! FBI! Son of a — *(He collapses in a heap. Blackout.)*

Scene 18

In darkness, the sound of televised hearings:

McCARTHY. *(V.O.)* Mr. Chairman?
CHAIRMAN. *(V.O.)* Senator McCarthy, it's late …
McCARTHY. *(V.O.)* I just need to say one more thing.
CHAIRMAN. *(V.O.)* The witness has already been excused.
McCARTHY. *(V.O.)* I'm done with the witness; I need to speak to the American public. *(Pause.)*
CHAIRMAN. *(V.O.)* Proceed.
McCARTHY. *(V.O.)* Some people have criticized me for trying to purge our State Department of the Red Menace. They accuse me of searching for Communists inside your closets and under your beds. *(Lights rise to reveal Mrs. Kravitz watching television.)* Well I have this to say to those critics: The Communist under your bed today is the Communist in your bed tomorrow. And your wife may decide not to tell you he's there. *(Pause.)*
CHAIRMAN. *(V.O.)* Um … thank you, Senator McCarthy.
ANNOUNCER. *(V.O.)* We will return to the hearings of the Senate Internal Security Subcommittee after these words from our sponsor. *(The Ogilby Kippers theme song kicks in. Andrei enters the apartment from outside. Mrs. Kravitz turns off the television.)*
MRS. KRAVITZ. There you are — I been worried sick. Did you

make the meeting?
ANDREI. I met someone, but not at meeting.
MRS. KRAVITZ. What do you — ? *(She sniffs him.)* You smell like a bar. Did you go to the pier?
ANDREI. Only person on pier was FBI man.
MRS. KRAVITZ. FBI?
ANDREI. Fishing like schoolboy and drinking like fish.
MRS. KRAVITZ. Did you say anything?
ANDREI. What can I say to FBI man? *(He gestures wildly:)* "At Lake Tahoe, I share clothes with Vincent Norman Peale."
MRS. KRAVITZ. At the bar, then.
ANDREI. I spoke only with pretty young lady looking for fiancé.
MRS. KRAVITZ. What about?
ANDREI. Leaky boats. *(He hands her Maggie's card.)*
MRS. KRAVITZ. Leaky … Christ Almighty. This is the cop — did she get a good look at you?
ANDREI. I told you, she was not looking for me.
MRS. KRAVITZ. Did she get a good look?
ANDREI. Yes. And I got good look at her. When I went back to pier, there was no one. *(Andrei takes off his coat.)*
MRS. KRAVITZ. Damn it to hell. There goes Guantánamo. And us with nothin but zeroes in the bank.
ANDREI. This meeting was not for money …
MRS. KRAVITZ. Don't start …
ANDREI. It was for keeping Olga living.
MRS. KRAVITZ. At this point, the meeting is moot, and you and me are up the creek. *(Silence. Finally, a lightbulb:)* Unless … *(Pause.)*
ANDREI. Unless what.
MRS. KRAVITZ. Unless there's a fallback meeting. *(Beat.)*
ANDREI. Fallback?
MRS. KRAVITZ. In case the first fell through.
ANDREI. When would be fallback?
MRS. KRAVITZ. How should I know? Nathan never told me anything outright. Could be tomorrow, could be a month.
ANDREI. Then I will wait, sleep in boat … *(He grabs his coat again.)*
MRS. KRAVITZ. No you won't. Not with agents around. I'll stop by tomorrow, and the next night, till we — *(There is a knock at the*

door. They freeze, then speak in hushed tones.) Did the cop follow you?
ANDREI. She leaved before me.
MRS. KRAVITZ. That means nothing. Did you even look behind you? *(Knocking.)*
LYNN. *(O.S.)* Mrs. Kravitz?
MRS. KRAVITZ. What do you want?
LYNN. *(O.S.)* It's me, Lynn.
MRS. KRAVITZ. Who?
LYNN. *(O.S.)* Lynn Mc — Jane! Jane Smith.
MRS. KRAVITZ. Christ, it's the girl from 2-A.
LYNN. *(O.S.)* I need to talk to you.
MRS. KRAVITZ. If you lost something, sorry, but I checked the room …
LYNN. *(O.S.)* No, no, it's not — can you open the door, please?
MRS. KRAVITZ. *(To Andrei.)* Make yourself scarce.
ANDREI. I am "Mr. Kravitz."
MRS. KRAVITZ. The less people see of you the better.
LYNN. *(O.S.)* Mrs. Kravitz?
MRS. KRAVITZ. Hold your horses, I gotta get a housecoat. *(To Andrei.)* Not a word.
ANDREI. Of course, no words. *(Mrs. Kravitz opens the door.)*
LYNN. I'm sorry to call so late, but I heard talking and — *(Seeing Andrei.)* Oh. Hello … *(Andrei signs elaborately.)* Uh …
MRS. KRAVITZ *(To Andrei.)* Of course, dear, don't stay up on account of us.
LYNN. Oh — good night. *(Andrei signs elaborately, aerobically. Pause.)* Um … *(She looks to Mrs. Kravitz.)*
MRS. KRAVITZ. You'll have to excuse my husband. He's got St. Vitus' Dance. *(Andrei gives her the finger, then stomps off. Pause.)* And Tourette's Syndrome — brutal combination. What do you want?
LYNN. I know I checked out this afternoon, but I need to stay a few extra nights.
MRS. KRAVITZ. I already filled your room.
LYNN. Both beds?
MRS. KRAVITZ. Two trawlers back from a twelve-week haul. I don't think you're up to it.
LYNN. I don't need the same room …
MRS. KRAVITZ. They're all filled, Missy. Busy time of year.

LYNN. Oh, no ...
MRS. KRAVITZ. You check out the Gull's Nest?
LYNN. Their sign said "No Vacancy."
MRS. KRAVITZ. So does mine.
LYNN. Oh dear, this is awful. *(She starts to cry.)*
MRS. KRAVITZ. Now there's no need to cry. I'm sure you'll find ... *(Lynn cries discreetly. Mrs. Kravitz regards her closely for a moment.)* This about your fella? The one you called?
LYNN. How did you know?
MRS. KRAVITZ. You were bawlin' then, too. *(Beat.)* Never marry a man who makes you cry. "Tears today, trouble tomorrow."
LYNN. That's what Aunt Pidge says.
MRS. KRAVITZ. Aunt Pidge is right. It might seem rosy till the honeymoon's over, but then a wife starts to notice things.
LYNN. Things?
MRS. KRAVITZ. You don't want to know.
LYNN. Yes I do. What kind of things?
MRS. KRAVITZ. Oh, say, a whiff of perfume, the hint of lipstick on a collar ...
LYNN. Oh.
MRS. KRAVITZ. The phony passports ...
LYNN. Phony passports?
MRS. KRAVITZ. The lethal weapon in his ascot drawer ...
LYNN. Why would your husband have a lethal weapon?
MRS. KRAVITZ. Exactly.
LYNN. Does Mr. — *(Sotto voce.)* Does Mr. Kravitz have a phony passport?
MRS. KRAVITZ. Let's not pry into the sanctity of marriage. Suffice it to say that a wife's job is to keep her own secrets and find out her husband's. *(Lynn ponders this. After a moment:)* Look, you seem like a good kid. I've got a room next to mine —
LYNN. I'll take it.
MRS. KRAVITZ. ... just ignore the sign on the door.
LYNN. What sign?
MRS. KRAVITZ. "Off-Limits — FBI."
LYNN. Oh!
MRS. KRAVITZ. One of my tenants bought the farm.
LYNN. He died?

MRS. KRAVITZ. Nothing contagious. If you don't want the room —
LYNN. No no, I'll take it. I have to. I don't have any choice …
MRS. KRAVITZ. *(Extending the key to her.)* Sometimes it's best that way, Missy. *(She drops it into her hand.)* Believe me, sometimes it's best that way. *(Blackout.)*

Scene 19

On the deck of a ship in the Marshall Islands. James, in uniform, stands between Dr. Kasden, a British physicist with clipboard and stopwatch, and Major Hartwell, a military lifer. All three look out, dark goggles over their eyes.

HARTWELL. This your first trip to the South Pacific, son?
JAMES. Yes sir.
HARTWELL. Beautiful place for an H-bomb test. Not every day you get to blow up paradise.
KASDEN. Heard you got a call from home last night, James.
JAMES. My fiancée.
HARTWELL. Bravo.
JAMES. Thank you, sir.
HARTWELL. I just talked to the wife myself.
KASDEN. How was it?
HARTWELL. She told me she's six weeks pregnant.
KASDEN. Congratulations!
HARTWELL. I been away the last four months. *(James and Kasden look at each other. Hartwell continues looking out.)* I say "How the hell did this happen?" She says she's walking the dog one morning, sees the neighbor's gate open, goes in, one thing leads to another …
KASDEN. Oh my.
HARTWELL. It conjures up an image.
JAMES. Yes sir.

HARTWELL. And me five thousand miles away doing my duty for God and country.
KASDEN. Then, the father is…?
HARTWELL. Mangy little poodle named Max. *(Beat.)*
JAMES. You mean to say…?
HARTWELL. Bow wow wow.
KASDEN. Oh my.
HARTWELL. Like I said, it conjures up an image.
JAMES. Yes sir. *(Pause.)*
HARTWELL. Took me ten minutes to figure out she was talking about our cocker spaniel, Maisy. *(Beat.)*
JAMES. Oh …
HARTWELL. Gonna have puppies any day now.
KASDEN. I assumed —
HARTWELL. Well, of course, who wouldn't? Goddamned phones have this weird delay …
JAMES. That happened to me, too, Major. Caused some confusion.
HARTWELL. Nothing of the canine sort, I hope…?
JAMES. No sir. No dogs.
HARTWELL. Good. Never did like poodles much. The thought of raising a litter as my own …
KASDEN. One minute remaining.
HARTWELL. Where's your fiancée?
JAMES. Wisconsin.
HARTWELL. Ah, Midwest girl. Be gentle with her.
JAMES. Sir?
HARTWELL. On your wedding night. Corn-fed girls tend to be "naive."
KASDEN. Major …
HARTWELL. Don't assume she's ever seen a grown man naked.
JAMES. Oh.
HARTWELL. Hell, when I stripped in front of Fern, you'd think she'd come face to face with King Kong. *(Beat.)*
JAMES. It conjures up an image, sir.
HARTWELL. Or has she already glimpsed you in a state of nature?
JAMES. I guess you could say that.
HARTWELL. Well done, Appel. And you were her first?

KASDEN. Major Hartwell, please …
HARTWELL. What.
KASDEN. You're embarrassing the boy.
HARTWELL. It's a reasonable question. You were her first, weren't you? *(Beat.)*
JAMES. Of course.
HARTWELL. Bravo. So who's keeping an eye on her while you're away?
JAMES. Sir?
HARTWELL. In the chastity department. There's no keeping them down on the farm once they've seen Paree.
JAMES. I think I can trust her.
HARTWELL. Lot of space between "think" and "trust."
JAMES. I trust her.
HARTWELL. Hear that, Dr. Kasden? Beautiful thing, young love. Me and Fern, we got a Cold War kind of trust. Based on the balance of power and a mutual fear of destruction.
KASDEN. Fifteen seconds.
HARTWELL. Just keep her out of the neighbor's yard, son. Nobody wants another man's puppies.
KASDEN. Ten … nine … eight … seven … six … turn around … *(They all turn their backs to the audience.)* four … three … two … one … *(As the count reaches zero, James turns around just as an intense white light floods the stage, followed by massive rumbling.)*
JAMES. *(Awed.)* My God … *(He whips off his goggles and looks out in wonder, then suddenly throws his hands over his eyes and drops to his knees, screaming.)* AAAAAAAAAAAAAARRRGGGHHH!!! *(In unison, Hartwell and Kasden look back and down at James as the rumbling continues. Blackout.)*

Scene 20

The hotel room. An empty bottle of whiskey leans against the tape recorder. Frank, in his underwear, has just awakened. He sits atop the unmade bed. Petey has just entered from outside, holding a sheet of paper.

PETEY. You been here all weekend?
FRANK. What day is it?
PETEY. Monday! *(Beat.)*
FRANK. At least I was on time for work …
PETEY. You musta been lit to the gills. Callin' me up at midnight …
FRANK. I called you?
PETEY. Twice! Ravin' about a girl, a box of Velveeta and a pelican …
FRANK. A pelican?
PETEY. Whatever you did, I don't want to know. *(Frank tries vainly to recall such an encounter.)* Anyway, I stopped by headquarters on the way in. *(He holds up a sheet of paper.)* Big News.
FRANK. What Big News?
PETEY. Hold onto your socks.
FRANK. What is it?
PETEY. Three guesses.
FRANK. Don't play with me, Pete. Is it good news or bad?
PETEY. I got the skinny on Olga Sergeevna. *(Beat.)*
FRANK. The boat?
PETEY. The wife. *(Frank snatches the paper from Petey and reads. Pause.)*
FRANK. Where did you get this?
PETEY. One of our boys in the Kremlin.
FRANK. He sure?
PETEY. He saw the documents himself.
FRANK. I guess the Reds never told Borchevsky …
PETEY. If they had, would he have kept spyin' for 'em? *(Petey takes back the paper.)* He must've been completely in the dark.

FRANK. Well, then, that makes two of us. *(Frank rises and starts getting dressed. Petey considers him for a moment before speaking.)*
PETEY. Listen, Frank — I'm sorry about what happened Friday … *(Frank does not respond.)* When you came back from City Hall, I thought there hadda be some mistake …
FRANK. Yeah, well. I guess some of us were just born to be bachelors.
PETEY. Don't give up. Number three'll be the charm.
FRANK. I don't recall seein' a line of women outside my door. Unless you're hopin' to fix me up with your one-legged cousin Dolores again.
PETEY. She's married now. *(Beat.)* When the right girl comes along —
FRANK. The right girl came along, Pete. They don't come righter than that. Too bad she already came with a husband. *(Beat.)* Anyway, marriage is overrated. What did it ever do for you but build up your tolerance for lousy coffee? *(There is a loud knocking at the door. Frank and Petey look at each other before Petey answers.)*
PETEY. Yeah?
MAGGIE. *(O.S.)* Petey, it's me. Is Frank there? *(Petey looks to Frank, who does not move.)* Frank? *(Pause. The knocking is now pounding.)* Frank?
FRANK. Frank went fishin'.
MAGGIE. *(O.S.)* Open up, wouldja?
FRANK. Deep sea fishin'.
MAGGIE. *(O.S.)* Don't play games with me.
FRANK. For squid.
MAGGIE. *(O.S.)* I swear, I'll kick the door in if I have to. *(Petey looks to Frank, but Frank remains motionless. The pounding becomes kicking. Frank sits and places the headphones over his ears. The loud kicking continues.)*
PETEY. Frank, she'll blow our cover. *(Frank doesn't move. The kicking continues. Finally, Petey opens the door.)*
MAGGIE. *(Entering.)* Hey, Pete. *(She takes in the bed, the room, and Frank, who does not acknowledge her.)*
Well, this explains a lot.
FRANK. Sorry, can't chat, I'm workin' on a case.
MAGGIE. So am I.

FRANK. Then I guess you haven't talked to your superiors …
MAGGIE. You know damn well / I have.
FRANK. See, I informed them yesterday morning—
MAGGIE. Will you look at me? *(Beat. Frank removes the headphones and continues calmly.)*
FRANK. I informed your superiors that, contrary to orders, you continued to investigate the Fish Pier murder.
MAGGIE. They suspended me.
FRANK. I told them your actions jeopardized our own investigation.
MAGGIE. I said they suspended / me! Don't you know what that means?
FRANK. I informed your superiors that *this is not a personal matter* … but rather one of security, trust —
MAGGIE. They took my badge, my weapon …
PETEY. I think I'll pick up some lunch … *(He moves discreetly toward the door.)*
MAGGIE. All they left me were the goddamn shoes!
FRANK. *(To Petey.)* Stay. *(Petey freezes.)*
MAGGIE. We should be working together.
FRANK. Why's that, Mrs. Murphy?
MAGGIE. We're partners.
FRANK. Petey and I are partners. Sit down. *(Petey sits down again.)*
MAGGIE. Did they match the prints in Washington?
FRANK. This is all about a case to you, isn't it?
MAGGIE. All I want to know is / did they —
FRANK. I informed your superiors —
MAGGIE. And I don't give a damn what you told my superiors!
PETEY. Maybe just Moxie and a can of kippers … *(Petey starts out again.)*
FRANK. Get some for me, too, wouldja, Pete? And show Mrs. Murphy out while you're at it … *(Frank sits and picks up the headphones as Petey opens the door.)*
MAGGIE. So you're jealous, is that it? *(Eyes still on Frank, Maggie shuts the door with one hand, keeping Petey in the room.)*
FRANK. Jealous?
MAGGIE. Of my husband.
FRANK. Why would I be jealous?

MAGGIE. Well, you keep throwin' his name around …
FRANK. Considerin' it's all I know about the man,—
MAGGIE. Fine, what do you want to know about him? What he drank? How he liked his eggs? Whether he was bigger, smaller, smarter, tougher than you? *(Frank puts the headphones on and turns his back to Maggie. She regards him for a long time, then continues, softer:)* First time he walked into the station was a couple months after V-J Day. Dressed like a dandy and wearin' a smile like it was some kinda secret weapon. *(She moves slowly toward Frank as she speaks.)* He said he was a writer — "gonna be the next Raymond Chandler," he said. Only he was sick of hardboiled cliches, needed to know what real crime's about, maybe I could help…? And there's that smile again … *(Beat. She reaches down and pulls the headphone jack from the tape recorder. Frank does not move.)* I'm still a rookie, wet behind the ears, still green. *(Beat.)* Still a virgin … *(Beat.)* So I start sneakin' files home, bring 'em back the next day. He copies details — reports, procedure — mundane stuff. Six weeks later we're headin' to City Hall, and I can just picture the dedication page of his hardcover debut: "For Marguerite, my wife, with love." *(Beat.)* Then I wake one fine spring morning to find one man and one file missing. *(Pause.)*
PETEY. One file?
MAGGIE. His. *(Off Petey's look:)* Zoltan Toth, Lester Tarabian, Sam Schmidt, Vito Rossi … a.k.a. Jack Murphy.
PETEY. You mean you were married to —
MAGGIE. When I agreed to take his name, I never guessed he had so many. *(Petey looks at Frank, then back to Maggie. Frank takes off the headphones but does not look at Maggie.)*
FRANK. *(Quietly.)* Why didn't you tell me?
MAGGIE. In five more months the law can declare him dead. I didn't think you needed to know. *(Pause.)*
FRANK. Well. Then I guess we both made mistakes. *(Frank rises wearily.)* Let me get the lunch, Pete. I could use some air …
MAGGIE. I'll come with you.
FRANK. Don't bother. *(To Petey.)* You and Peggy ready for a second honeymoon?
PETEY. Huh?
FRANK. Here you go. *(He hands an envelope to Petey.)*

MAGGIE. Frank …
PETEY. "Honeymoon"?
FRANK. Havana.
PETEY. Aw, no.
FRANK. Boat leaves tomorrow night.
PETEY. I couldn't.
FRANK. Sure you can. I'll hold down the fort. *(He starts out.)*
MAGGIE. *(To Frank.)* Don't go.
PETEY. I mean it, I can't take these!
FRANK. Adios, Margarita. *(He exits. Petey calls after him:)*
PETEY. I'm terrified of boats! *(Long pause. Maggie moves away from the door.)* I'm sorry, Maggie. Really I am. I mean, you two were made for each other. You're broke in all the same places.
MAGGIE. Did they match the prints in Washington? *(Beat.)*
PETEY. *(Moving away.)* Why don't you ask McCloskey?
MAGGIE. As you may have noticed, I don't have carte blanche down at the station.
PETEY. Then it's not my place to say.
MAGGIE. So don't say anything;
PETEY. Maggie …
MAGGIE. just nod if it's yes, shake your head if it's —
PETEY. Why do you need to know?
MAGGIE. Because Andrei's alive. *(Pause.)*
PETEY. Andrei?
MAGGIE. Friday night at Duffy's we shared a glass of vodka. He picked up the vodka; I picked up the glass. *(She pulls out a shotglass.)*
PETEY. How do you know —
MAGGIE. These prints matched everything in his apartment.
PETEY. Wait a second …
MAGGIE. Now what about the ones we sent to Washington?
PETEY. Hold on …
MAGGIE. *Did they match them?*
PETEY. Maggie …
MAGGIE. Did they match them?
PETEY. Yeah, but they were totally useless!
MAGGIE. Why?
PETEY. They came up with nine different guys. Some rookie must've screwed up the match.

MAGGIE. Nine different guys?
PETEY. McCloskey sent 'em right back. *(Noting the look on her face:)* Nine different guys?! *(She nods. Blackout.)*

Scene 21

A Catholic confessional in a shadowy church. Perhaps the glow of stained glass. Lynn enters the area, crosses herself, and enters the confessional. A Priest opens the screened window.

LYNN. Bless me, Father, it's been eight days since my last confession.
PRIEST. What are your sins?
LYNN. Well, once I lied to my fiancé, once I lied to my mother about my fiancé, and once I seduced my fiancé by reenacting an erotic dream. *(Beat.)*
PRIEST. Go on …
LYNN. Also, I had impure thoughts a hundred and eighteen times. Not including the dream.
PRIEST. My, my. Well, for your penance —
LYNN. A hundred and nineteen times.
PRIEST. Excuse me?
LYNN. I just remembered the dream.
PETEY. I see. For your penance —
LYNN. One twenty.
PRIEST. Stop that.
LYNN. I'm trying, but I just keep picturing this rowboat, and one twenty-one.
PRIEST. I mean stop counting. An estimate will do.
LYNN. Yes, Father. *(Andrei enters furtively, crosses himself, and enters the other side of the confessional.)*
PRIEST. For your penance, do the sorrowful mysteries of the rosary.
LYNN. Thank you, Father.
PRIEST. Say an Act of Contrition.
LYNN. Before you absolve me, can I confess something else?

PRIEST. But of course.
LYNN. I guess what I need to know is, can I confess something I haven't done yet?
PRIEST. Well ... rather than confess it, maybe you simply shouldn't do it.
LYNN. Oh, but I can't not do it. *(Impatient, Andrei knocks at the other window.)* What was that?
PRIEST. Nothing. You were saying?
LYNN. I was saying I have to do this, it means so much to him. It's just that I feel so guilty ... *(Beat.)*
PRIEST. Is it a number?
LYNN. My mother said the same thing ... *(Andrei knocks again, more insistent.)* Is that someone knocking? *(Beat.)*
PRIEST. Just a moment. *(The Priest shuts Lynn's window and opens Andrei's.)* Yes?
ANDREI. Bless me, Father, I am six years without —
PRIEST. Excuse me, but I'm already with someone, you'll have to wait. *(The Priest shuts Andrei's window and opens Lynn's.)* Sorry about that. Continue.
LYNN. A hundred twenty-two.
PRIEST. What?
LYNN. The rowboat dream again. See, he asked me to do this thing — and I'll do it, I love him too much to say no. I just don't know if I can marry a man who would ask me to do something I could only do if I loved him too much to say no. You know?
PRIEST. Marriage is a mystery.
LYNN. Then there's the whole thing about the baby. *(Andrei knocks again.)*
PRIEST. Baby?
LYNN. I'm pregnant. Oh, but it's not his baby, it's somebody else's.
PRIEST. Why didn't you mention this before?
LYNN. I was absolved for the baby last week. *(Andrei knocks.)* Is that person going to keep knocking like that? *(Beat.)*
PRIEST. Excuse me. *(He shuts her window and opens Andrei's.)*
ANDREI. Bless me, Father —
PRIEST. I told you once, I'm with someone else.
ANDREI. But — *(The Priest shuts Andrei's window and opens Lynn's.)*
PRIEST. Pardon me.

LYNN. One twenty-three, so I figured if I — *(Andrei knocks. The Priest shuts Lynn's window and opens Andrei's.)*
ANDREI. Bless me —
PRIEST. Look, do you want absolution or not?
ANDREI. I need to speak with you.
PRIEST. Fine, I'll be with you as soon as I'm done.
ANDREI. I'm killing myself. *(The Priest shuts Andrei's window, then reconsiders and reopens it.)*
PRIEST. What did you say?
ANDREI. Bless me, Father, I am six years without a confession.
PRIEST. Did you say —
ANDREI. Many times I am having impure thoughts, many times I take Lord's name in vain. I have slept with wife of another man on forty or fifty occasions, and once I lied to a priest.
PRIEST. And because of these sins you would take your own life?
ANDREI. No, that was the lie. *(Beat.)*
PRIEST. If you deliberately deceive me — *(Impatient, Lynn knocks from the other side.)*
ANDREI. I would not be here, but Mrs. Kravitz says I am dead —
PRIEST. Just wait five minutes —
ANDREI. ... I cannot speak, I cannot be seen ... *(Lynn knocks again, harder.)*
PRIEST. Hold on.
ANDREI. Don't ... *(The Priest shuts Andrei's window and opens Lynn's.)*
LYNN. I thought this place was first-come, first-served.
PRIEST. Forgive me.
LYNN. See, I really need some advice ... If I deliver this thing tomorrow night, I — *(Andrei knocks again.)*
PRIEST. For God's sake ...
LYNN. Wait! *(But the Priest shuts her window and opens Andrei's.)*
PRIEST. I must ask you to step outside the confessional until — *(Lynn bangs on her window.)* Until such time as I have finished — *(Lynn bangs. The Priest closes Andrei's door and opens Lynn's.)* What? *(Andrei bangs.)* Urgh! *(He shuts Lynn's and opens Andrei's.)* Stop it! *(Lynn bangs. The Priest opens her side as well.)* Stop it this instant! *(He shuts both sides, crosses himself, and takes a deep breath. Pause. They both begin pounding simultaneously.)* Enough! Enough! *(In exaspera-*

tion, he slides both windows back and stands.) You can live with your sins! I don't absolve either of you of anything! *(The Priest storms off.)*
LYNN. Wait, come back! I wasn't finished! *(Pause.)* Hello? *(Pause. To herself:)* Are they allowed to do that?
ANDREI. I don't know, I am Orthodox.
LYNN. You! This is all your fault!
ANDREI. I am sorry.
LYNN. Banging like a Fuller Brush Man ...
ANDREI. I have desperate problem;
LYNN. Well join the club.
ANDREI. ... but no one can I talk to. *(Beat.)* There is person I love, who I want to marry, but ... *(Beat.)* Conscience will not let me. *(Pause. Lynn becomes cautiously curious.)*
LYNN. Why not?
ANDREI. She wants me to do something I cannot do. *(Pause.)*
LYNN. Is it a number? *(Beat.)*
ANDREI. What do you mean?
LYNN. I have no idea, I was hoping you'd know. *(Pause.)* The person I want to marry also wants me to do something I can't do.
ANDREI. What is this thing?
LYNN. You expect me to tell you?
ANDREI. It is dark ...
LYNN. A perfect stranger?
ANDREI. Priest was stranger also.
LYNN. At least he was a priest. You're just a ... rude person with an accent.
ANDREI. Not for absolution. No one can give absolution. Only, maybe, understanding. This, perhaps, we can give. *(Pause.)*
LYNN. Well ... my fiance ... *(Pause.)* I haven't told anyone about this ...
ANDREI. Please. I am used to keeping mouth shut. *(Beat.)*
LYNN. He wants me to deliver ... something.
ANDREI. Something.
LYNN. Blueprints. For a bomb. *(Pause.)*
ANDREI. I see.
LYNN. I didn't even know he was a spy till after — I shouldn't be telling you this ...
ANDREI. When do you need to deliver this blueprints?

LYNN. Tomorrow night, / but —
ANDREI. At same location? *(Beat.)*
LYNN. What do you mean "same location"?
ANDREI. Some.
LYNN. What?
ANDREI. Some location, you will deliver at some location, yes? *(Beat.)*
LYNN. I think I've told you enough … *(Lynn swiftly and silently rises and exits.)*
ANDREI. Of course. No need to say any more. The point is, you love this man, so you must deliver his blueprints at fallback meeting. There is no question. Then you will marry and have some babies and everyone is happy, yes? *(Beat.)* Yes? *(Beat. Fearing she has slipped out, Andrei jumps out and opens Lynn's confessional door, but she is gone.)*

Scene 22

The morgue. Maggie and Harry, now in casual dress, his jacket covered in "Ike" buttons. On the gurney sits a plain metal canister.

HARRY. Apparently nobody told you government workers get Election Day off.
MAGGIE. Sorry — I needed to see him again.
HARRY. Apparently they also didn't say you've been suspended. *(Pause.)*
MAGGIE. Where is he?
HARRY. There. *(He gestures to the canister. Beat.)*
MAGGIE. You mean…?
HARRY. Ashes to ashes. *(Maggie is stunned.)* We can only keep them so long.
MAGGIE. I was hoping to look in his eyes one last time.
HARRY. Take a look. They're in there somewhere. *(Maggie picks*

up the can and opens it.) You vote today?
MAGGIE. Hmm? No, I … forgot.
HARRY. Looks like a landslide. Finally, an elephant in the White House after twenty years of jackasses …
MAGGIE. Is that the autopsy report?
HARRY. What do you need to know?
MAGGIE. The contents of his stomach.
HARRY. If you're hopin' for more loose change …
MAGGIE. I mean his last supper. Was it herring?
HARRY. I'm a coroner, not an ichthyologist.
MAGGIE. Fish, then. Could you tell if it was fish? *(Beat. Harry looks in the file folder, flips a page, stops, then looks up.)*
HARRY. Lucky guess, right? *(Maggie shuts her eyes and clamps the lid back onto the canister.)* After all, he was a fisherman …
MAGGIE. Can I take him with me?
HARRY. What?
MAGGIE. The ashes.
HARRY. No!
MAGGIE. Why not?
HARRY. Why?
MAGGIE. It's important.
HARRY. You know the rules, Maggie: / only family —
MAGGIE. "Only family," I know.
HARRY. Then how can you —
MAGGIE. He's my husband. *(Blackout.)*

Scene 23

Mrs. Kravitz at her apartment door, Frank outside.

FRANK. I wanna talk to Mr. Kravitz.
MRS. KRAVITZ. He doesn't talk.
FRANK. Then I wanna see him whirl like a dervish, 'cause I've got questions. Where is he? *(He moves past her into the apartment,*

disappearing into other rooms.)
MRS. KRAVITZ. Out.
FRANK. *(O.S.)* Out where?
MRS. KRAVITZ. He didn't leave an itinerary. *(Frank reenters.)*
FRANK. Let me into Andrei's place.
MRS. KRAVITZ. Haven't you poked through his things enough?
FRANK. I'm not lookin' for his things, I'm lookin' for him.
MRS. KRAVITZ. Then visit the morgue.
FRANK. Where are the keys?
MRS. KRAVITZ. *(Pulling her keys out.)* I shoulda put in a turnstile … *(The two cross over into "Andrei's apartment." Frank becomes a bloodhound, poking his nose everywhere.)* Anything I can do to make you feel more at home? Pipe? Slippers?
FRANK. You know how to make a stiff drink? *(He exits into a side room.)*
MRS. KRAVITZ. Feed him salty snacks. *(Pause. Frank returns.)*
FRANK. If you think I'm here to play Burns to your Allen, you're mistaken. What did you do with his slicker and boots?
MRS. KRAVITZ. What do you mean?
FRANK. Where are they?
MRS. KRAVITZ. In his closet.
FRANK. Guess again. *(Beat. Mrs. Kravitz exits. Pause.)*
MRS. KRAVITZ. *(O.S.)* Goddamn, goddamn, SON OF A BITCH! *(Beat. Mrs. Kravitz reenters, outwardly calm.)* Nathan musta borrowed 'em. It's his bridge night.
FRANK. He went to play bridge on a clear night wearin' an oilskin mackintosh and hip boots?
MRS. KRAVITZ. That man has no sense of fashion.
FRANK. Where's your putative husband, Mrs. Kravitz? *(Frank begins rooting through the trash can again.)*
MRS. KRAVITZ. Don't you call my husband names.
FRANK. Out sellin' secret weapons informa — *(He stops dead, reaches for something in the trash can.)* Holy …
MRS. KRAVITZ. What, what is it?
FRANK. *(To himself.)* Well I'll be jiggered … *(He pulls out a ring and reads the inscription.)*
MRS. KRAVITZ. That ring belongs to a tenant.
FRANK. There is a Velveeta girl …

MRS. KRAVITZ. You can't just — anything left in the room is mine!
FRANK. Oh, I'm not gonna keep the ring, Mrs. Kravitz. This inscription's all I need. *(He starts out.)*
MRS. KRAVITZ. Inscription? Wait — what inscription? *(Frank turns back.)*
FRANK. Let's just say it doesn't add up to eight. *(Blackout.)*

Scene 24

The docks. Night. A light glows inside Andrei's boat. Lynn enters wearing sunglasses, as before. She looks about nervously, awaiting her unknown contact. A slickered fisherman appears on the boat or dock, arranging items for the next voyage. Lynn conceals herself, watching him carefully. Finally, seeing no one else nearby, she calls out to him:

LYNN. Hello? *(The slickered man stops and looks out.)* Excuse me, are you by any chance … waiting … for somebody?
ANDREI. That depends on who are you.
LYNN. Somebody. *(The man approaches. Lynn moves a few feet away.)*
ANDREI. Did you bring it?
LYNN. Bring what?
ANDREI. What you are supposed to bring.
LYNN. What might that be?
ANDREI. The … item.
LYNN. Which item?
ANDREI. The item you are bringing! *(As he advances, Lynn backs up.)*
LYNN. Wait a minute …
ANDREI. Why do you play games?
LYNN. That accent …
ANDREI. We must hurry!
LYNN. You're the man from confession! *(Beat.)*
ANDREI. *(Removing his hood.)* I confess I am that man …

LYNN. You heard everything I said — oh my God, Mr. Kravitz?
ANDREI. Who?
LYNN. What are you doing here? Did Mrs. Kravitz send you?
ANDREI. *Oh ...*
LYNN. I never told her —
ANDREI. Miss Smith!
LYNN. Who?
ANDREI. You are Miss Smith, from 2-A!
LYNN. Wait ...
ANDREI. Jane Smith, yes?
LYNN. You can speak ...
ANDREI. What?
LYNN. You're talking, I thought you had to ... *(She attempts a faltering sign language.)*
ANDREI. Yes. Well. Miraculous cure. Now please, miss — the item, quickly ... *(He steps forward, she backs up.)*
LYNN. "A wonderful bird is the pelican." *(Beat.)*
ANDREI. What?
LYNN. *(Deliberately.)* "A wonderful bird is the pelican ... "
ANDREI. So?
LYNN. Goodbye. *(She turns to go.)*
ANDREI. Wait ...
LYNN. I have to go now ...
ANDREI. If this is code, I don't know code ...
LYNN. Let go of me ...
ANDREI. But I am somebody you wait for!
LYNN. Let go or I'll scream ...
ANDREI. Please, Miss Smith —
LYNN. Help!
ANDREI. Give me the item!
LYNN. Help me! *(Seeing force will not work, Andrei releases her and tries to play the game:)*
ANDREI. Pelican bird is wonderful bird!
LYNN. Why? *(Pause.)* Why? *(Beat.)*
ANDREI. *(Helpless.)* I don't know. *(Lynn starts out but is blocked by Mrs. Kravitz. Lynn gasps in surprise.)*
MRS. KRAVITZ. His bill will hold more than his belican.
ANDREI. Mrs. Kravitz...?

MRS. KRAVITZ. Ogden Nash, right?
LYNN. What?
MRS. KRAVITZ. "His bill will hold more than his belican ... "?
LYNN. Oh —
ANDREI. I had to make meeting.
LYNN. "He can take in his beak ... "
MRS. KRAVITZ. "Food enough for a week ... "
LYNN. "But I'm damned if I see how the helican."
MRS. KRAVITZ. Where is it?
ANDREI. I must save Olga. *(Lynn pulls out the cheese.)*
MRS. KRAVITZ. Give it to me.
ANDREI. No, don't.
MRS. KRAVITZ. Stay out of this.
ANDREI. A woman's life is at stake! *(Lynn, frightened, backs away from both of them.)*
MRS. KRAVITZ. Don't listen to him ...
ANDREI. My wife is rotting in Soviet gulag!
MRS. KRAVITZ. For all you know, she's rotting in a grave!
ANDREI. No!
MRS. KRAVITZ. Why would Nathan give a shit about Olga?
ANDREI. *(To Lynn.)* Please ...
MRS. KRAVITZ. He lied and kept the cash for himself.
ANDREI. Give me the item.
MRS. KRAVITZ. Don't.
LYNN. You're confusing me ...
MRS. KRAVITZ. Hand it over! *(Mrs. Kravitz and Andrei reach for the Velveeta box. Lynn screams, tosses it high in the air, and bolts. Andrei and Mrs. Kravitz scramble for it. But Frank has appeared, packing a formidable-looking shotgun.)*
FRANK. All right, freeze, I wanna see statues!
LYNN. Oh!
ANDREI. Oh no ...
MRS. KRAVITZ. Oh Christ, it's him.
FRANK. Glad you folks could make it tonight. I'm especially glad the cat gave back your tongue, "Mr. Kravitz." Truly the Power of Positive Thinking.
LYNN. Can I just say one thing?
FRANK. First I need someone to hand me that yellow box.

LYNN. I don't know these people.
MRS. KRAVITZ. The hell you don't.
LYNN. We just met!
FRANK. We've got all night for denials and confessions. First the cheese. *(Mrs. Kravitz brings Frank the cheese. Frank slips a handcuff on her right wrist, then takes it.)* Thanks. Who's next?
ANDREI. Please, sir ...
FRANK. Good — a volunteer.
ANDREI. This box spares the life of a person ...
FRANK. Put your wrist in the other cuff.
ANDREI. It is saving my wife!
FRANK. I'm afraid you're too late to save Olga Sergeevna. *(Beat.)*
MRS. KRAVITZ. "Too late"? *(Beat.)*
ANDREI. *(Quietly.)* She is dead, then?
FRANK. The Reds released her two years ago. She's happily married and livin' in Moscow. *(He cuffs Andrei's left wrist.)*
ANDREI. "Married"?
FRANK. When you never came back, she had you declared dead. *(Pulling out a second pair of cuffs.)* You're next, Miss.
ANDREI. Everyone declares me dead ...
FRANK. Sorry about that.
ANDREI. I am not dead!
FRANK. Miss. *(He cuffs Andrei's right wrist.)*
LYNN. You can't do this to me ...
FRANK. Where'd you come across this box?
LYNN. I want to talk to a lawyer first.
FRANK. I'll bet it wasn't in the dairy case.
LYNN. My father's a very important person.
FRANK. I'm sure.
LYNN. His name is Joseph McCarthy. *(Beat.)*
MRS. KRAVITZ. You're Joe McCarthy's daughter?
LYNN. That's right.
FRANK. Yeah. And I was engaged to Ethel Mirman ... *(Frank cuffs Lynn's left wrist to Andrei's right.)*
LYNN. I am!
FRANK. Now who's your contact at Los Alamos?
LYNN. I don't know what you're talking about, and I resent the very implication that I might be involved with something illegal ...

(Suddenly, a familiar voice calls from the distance:)
JAMES. *(O.S.)* Lynn! *(Lynn looks out, incredulous.)*
FRANK *(To Lynn.)* Who's that?
JAMES. *(O.S.)* It's me!
LYNN. This is not my week ...
JAMES. *(O.S.)* Can you hear me?
LYNN. James?
JAMES. *(O.S.)* I found you! Just in time!
FRANK. *(Pointing the shotgun offstage.)* All right, hands up!
JAMES. *(O.S.)* I can't believe it!
LYNN. Turn around! Turn around and run! *(James stumbles onto the dock wearing his uniform and dark sunglasses. He carries a white cane.)*
JAMES. Where are you?
FRANK. Hold it right there.
LYNN. Don't say anything, just — what happened to your eyes?
JAMES. Don't worry ...
LYNN. Oh my God, you're blind ... *(Frank, confused, lowers the shotgun.)*
JAMES. They said it's only temporary.
LYNN. Darling!
JAMES. Don't give it to them — where are you?
LYNN. Over here, but — *
JAMES. I just want to hold you. *(He rushes toward the sound of her voice and misses completely.)*
LYNN. Look out for the — *(James disappears off the edge of the dock.)* James! *(There is a loud "splash!" To Frank.)* Don't just stand there, help him! James?
JAMES. *(O.S.)* I'm all right!
LYNN. There's a ladder in front of you.
JAMES. *(O.S.)* What?
LYNN. A ladder, right in fro — Just follow my voice.
MRS. KRAVITZ. *(To Andrei.)* They don't make spies like they used to ...
LYNN. That's it ... *(James climbs up the side of the dock, soaking wet, sunglasses akilter, still holding his cane.)*
JAMES. I saw it, baby lamb. I saw the light. *
LYNN. Don't talk, darling, there are people here ...

---

* See Note on Alternative Text on page 102.

JAMES. I don't care.
LYNN. Oh, but you will.
JAMES. It was like some terrible sunrise, burning up the sky. That's what fried my retinas — only temporary, they said.
LYNN. Sweetheart ...
JAMES. And I knew we had to be married. Because *fusion is stronger than fission.*
LYNN. What are you talking about?
JAMES. Joining together is a thousand times more powerful than splitting apart.
LYNN. James ...
JAMES. Forget the microfilm! Where is it? Throw it in the ocean now, before it's too late!
LYNN. Bunny ...
JAMES. It's death, and all that matters is life — you, me, and our love, forever!
LYNN. It's already too late. *(Beat.)*
JAMES. What do you mean?
FRANK. Special Agent Keller, Federal Bureau of Investigation. *(Pause.)*
JAMES. Oh.
FRANK. Glad we waited. I'd hate to have made you miss the boat. If I could borrow your right hand, Mrs. Kravitz ... *(Frank unlocks Andrei from her right handcuff.)*
JAMES. Lynn?
LYNN. I tried to tell you ...
FRANK. As a law keeper I must inform you that you will be held on federal conspiracy charges.
JAMES. Oh God ...
FRANK. But as a man I feel obliged to add that this woman's no longer your fiancée.
JAMES. What?
LYNN. How dare you!
FRANK. *(To Lynn.)* It's customary, when rejecting a proposal, to return the ring.
JAMES. What's he talking about?
FRANK. Why else would she dispose of her diamond in a boardinghouse litter can?

JAMES. She wouldn't!
FRANK. Oh no?
JAMES. Tell him, Lynn.
LYNN. Um ...
JAMES. Tell him our love is infinite! *(Frank removes the ring from his pocket and places it in James' hand.)*
FRANK. I hate to tell you, but the math is wrong. *(Pause. James is devastated.)*
JAMES. Lynn?
LYNN. Maybe this isn't the best place to talk ...
FRANK. Now — can I have your left hand, Mr....?
LYNN. Don't tell him.
JAMES. Appel.
FRANK. Thank you. *(Frank cuffs James' left hand to Mrs. Kravitz.)*
JAMES. Ow! *(He drops his cane.)*
FRANK. There we go. Two by two, like Noah's ark. All right, ladies and gentlemen, let's proceed calmly and carefully down the dock.
JAMES. *(Groping with his free hand.)* Excuse me...?
FRANK. Yeah?
JAMES. Could I have my cane back?
FRANK. Sure. *(Frank bends down for the cane and hands it to James.)* Here you gOOOOH — *(Mrs. Kravitz slams him in the groin with her foot. With her free hand, she grabs the shotgun, and slams the butt of it into Frank's face. Lynn screams; Frank collapses.)*
JAMES. What? What happened?
MRS. KRAVITZ. *(Training the shotgun on Frank.)* Sorry to knock in your pebbles —
JAMES. Oh ...
MRS. KRAVITZ. ... but a girl's gotta do what a girl just did.
LYNN. Was that really necessary?
MRS. KRAVITZ. Unless you and soldier-boy want to wind up like the Rosenbergs. *(Frank groans and starts crawling slowly and painfully away.)* Listen, Keller — you pass me the keys to these handcuffs or I'll take them from a dead man.
JAMES. Oh God ...
ANDREI. Stop please, Mr. FBI ... *(Frank continues crawling.)*
MRS. KRAVITZ. Not another inch!
LYNN. Don't shoot him!

ANDREI. Once this woman makes up her mind …
LYNN. James, do something!
JAMES. I can't even see! *(James throws up his hands, yanking the shotgun towards Lynn and Andrei, who scream and duck.)*
MRS. KRAVITZ. *(To James.)* Hold still!
ANDREI. Please, Mr. Keller …
MRS. KRAVITZ. All right, have it your way. *(She cocks the shotgun.)*
LYNN. No!
JAMES. Don't do it!
ANDREI. *(To Mrs. Kravitz.)* Look out! *(For Maggie has entered in stockinged feet behind Mrs. Kravitz. Before Mrs. Kravitz can turn around, Maggie jams an unseen weapon into her back. In the other hand, she holds the metal canister.)*
MAGGIE. Easy on the trigger, Mrs. Kravitz.
MRS. KRAVITZ. What the…?
MAGGIE. You put a shell into his back, I put one into yours.
ANDREI. *(Recognizing her.)* You …
MAGGIE. I can overlook your killin' my husband; killin' my lover's gonna tick me off.
MRS. KRAVITZ. "Husband"? What are you —
MAGGIE. Jack Murphy. Also known as Zoltan Toth, Lester Tarabian, Moby Dick, Hermes … and Nathan Kravitz.
FRANK. Nathan Kravitz?
LYNN. *(Pointing to Andrei.)* He's Nathan Kravitz …
JAMES. Who's Nathan Kravitz?
MAGGIE. This is Nathan Kravitz. *(She tosses the metal canister onto the pier with a clunk. Everyone looks at it.)*
FRANK. I pictured him taller.
MAGGIE. The Mercury dime was a nice touch. I guess you didn't miss it in *True Detective* after all. Now hand me that weapon, nice and slow. *(Pause.)* Not that slow.
ANDREI. Do it, Mrs. Kravitz. *(She looks at him.)* It is over. *(Mrs. Kravitz hands the shotgun to Maggie, who backs up and considers the shoe in her other hand.)*
MAGGIE. Damn shoes finally came in handy for something … *(She tosses it aside.)*
LYNN. What?
MRS. KRAVITZ. Oh, for Chrissake … *(Frank stands unsteadily.)*

JAMES. Could somebody tell me what's going on?
MAGGIE. Hi, Frank.
FRANK. Hey, Mag.
MAGGIE. Is that a fish in your pocket, or are you just glad to see me?
FRANK. What are you doin' here?
MAGGIE. Your "partner"'s on my honeymoon; somebody had to watch your back.
FRANK. Did you bring cuffs?
MAGGIE. *(Pointedly.)* I'm not a cop this week, remember?
MRS. KRAVITZ. Not a cop?
MAGGIE. Besides, if I weren't suspended, I'd have to arrest somebody.
MRS. KRAVITZ. You mean to say — ?
FRANK. *(Pulling out his pistol.)* Don't worry, Mrs. Kravitz. I'm perfectly capable of hauling you all in myself.
JAMES. Sir —
FRANK. *(To all.)* All right —
JAMES. I think you should let Lynn go.
FRANK. What you think is irrelevant.
JAMES. Please — you've already got me.
LYNN. Bunny!
ANDREI. Let Mrs. Kravitz go, too.
LYNN. And James.
FRANK. Hey —
MRS. KRAVITZ. Andrei never killed anybody.
FRANK. I don't remember callin' for a vote.
MAGGIE. Will you marry me? *(Beat. All heads turn towards Maggie.)*
FRANK. What?
MAGGIE. Will you, Frank?
JAMES. I'm confused.
MAGGIE. I don't need a ring, or a buncha white froufrou. But we belong together. Like a pair of bum shoes.
FRANK. I'm tryin' to arrest people.
MAGGIE. Sounds like they belong together too. *(To Lynn:)* The one with the sunglasses your fiancé?
LYNN. Well …

JAMES. I was. Until tonight ...
MAGGIE. And you, Mrs. Kravitz — this your "mute" husband?
ANDREI. I am not mute!
MRS. KRAVITZ. Don't get him started ...
ANDREI. Everybody says I am mute!
FRANK. All right, we're wastin' time, get movin' ...
MAGGIE. You haven't answered my question.
FRANK. *What.*
MAGGIE. *Will you marry me? (Beat.)*
FRANK. *(Brushing it aside.)* Fine, okay, we'll head down tomorrow ...
MAGGIE. Tonight.
FRANK. Huh?
MAGGIE. Here. Now.
FRANK. Are you out of your gourd?
MAGGIE. Tonight I finally became a widow; tonight I finally want to feel like a wife. Your wife — bailin' out our little boat together.
FRANK. Well, you'll notice I'm a little bit busy tonight ...
MAGGIE. *(To Andrei.)* Is it true a ship's captain can marry two people?
FRANK. Maggie ...
ANDREI. No, just one, like everybody else. *(Pause.)*
MAGGIE. Let me rephrase the question:
ANDREI. You are thinking of Mormons ...
JAMES. It's a myth. Ship's captains can't ordain a marriage.
FRANK. Sure they can.
JAMES. I checked it out. It has to be a clergyman, judge, or justice of the peace.
MAGGIE. That's it?
FRANK. Good, we're gonna see a judge in half an hour ... *(He tries to move them along again.)*
JAMES. Unless ...
LYNN. Unless what?
JAMES. *(Gradually realizing the possibilities.)* Unless ... it's a Quaker wedding ...
MRS. KRAVITZ. Quaker?
JAMES. Yeah — then you just marry each other. In front of your friends and your God.
LYNN. Is that legal?

JAMES. It's perfectly legal.
FRANK. Speakin' of legal, you're all under arrest.
MAGGIE. For what?
FRANK. How about first-degree murder, conspiracy, espionage, and kickin' a government agent in the balls?
MAGGIE. I don't see any murderers here. Just a thoughtful wife who fixed her husband a home-cooked meal that happened to asphyxiate him. What was the recipe, Mrs. Kravitz? Herring is such a versatile fish.
MRS. KRAVITZ. I call it "Herring Surprise."
MAGGIE. Good name.
FRANK. And what do you call this? *(He holds aloft the Velveeta.)*
MAGGIE. A box of cheese.
LYNN. It's not real cheese ...
FRANK. The H-bomb plans are inside.
MAGGIE. How do you know?
FRANK. You want me to open it up?
MAGGIE. No, I want you to toss it in the harbor.
FRANK. Toss it?
MAGGIE. Then I want to get married.
FRANK. This is my only evidence!
MAGGIE. If you toss it now, it'll always be just a box of cheese.
LYNN. But it's not cheese, see —
FRANK and MAGGIE. Shut up.
MAGGIE. You've already kept the Reds from gettin' it ...
FRANK. But what about these guys?
MAGGIE. They want to get married, too. *(Beat. Lynn turns to James, Mrs. Kravitz to Andrei.)* Isn't that what this was all about?
FRANK. Aw no, enough happy talk, let's go ... *(He moves to escort the others off the dock.)*
MAGGIE. Hold on ...
FRANK. Everybody out to the truck! *(Maggie stops them all with the shotgun.)*
MAGGIE. Nobody's movin' an inch.
FRANK. What?!
MAGGIE. My gun's bigger than yours.
FRANK. You're obstructin' a federal case!
MAGGIE. So what are you gonna do, arrest me? You ran out of cuffs.

MRS. KRAVITZ. She's got you there. *(Frank glares at Mrs. Kravitz.)*
MAGGIE. *(Of James:)* This one's never gonna spy again; and she only helped him because she's carryin' another man's baby. *(Lynn gasps.)*
JAMES. Baby?
MAGGIE. *(To Lynn.)* Sorry.
JAMES. What baby?
LYNN. Um …
MAGGIE. *(Of Andrei.)* This man did it to save his wife so he could be free to marry a woman who killed her husband to be with him.
FRANK. I'll make sure they go on trial together. *(He tries to move them along, but Maggie stops him again:)*
MAGGIE. You solved your case, Frank. Caught your fish. Now it's time to throw it back.
FRANK. Why are you tryin' so hard to trip me up?
MAGGIE. Maybe because they're a little like us: fumblin', fightin', makin' mistakes. Two ordinary people in an imperfect world who happen to love each other somethin' fierce. *(Beat. Frank looks down at the Velveeta box and makes a last vain argument:)*
FRANK. I spent two years on this …
MAGGIE. And I spent seven tryin' to harpoon a white whale. *(She picks up the canister of ashes.)* Turned out he was just a red herring. *(She moves to Frank.)* Come on, Frank. The honeymoon's over — let's get married. *(Pause.)*
FRANK. Sure. What the hell. *(They kiss. Beat.)*
JAMES. Does this mean we're not under arrest? *(Maggie and Frank move to the edge of the dock. In unison, they drop the canister and Velveeta box into the harbor with a splash.)*
LYNN. James …
ANDREI. Mrs. Kravitz …
LYNN. Do you still want me?
ANDREI. You will be my wife?
JAMES. Of course — I'm going to be a father …
MRS. KRAVITZ. Only if you stop calling me Mrs. Kravitz.
MAGGIE. So. This Quaker wedding. How's it work?
JAMES. Oh — I … hope I can remember … *(Music fades in as the three couples move into a rough semicircle, those in handcuffs*

interlocking so as to be next to their partners.) Repeat after me: In the presence of God …
OTHERS. In the presence of God …
JAMES. And these our … friends …
OTHERS. And these our friends … *(Lights begin to fade down as the billboard begins to fade up.)*
JAMES. I take thee Lynn …
OTHERS. I take thee …
MAGGIE. Frank …
MRS. KRAVITZ. Andrei …
LYNN. James …
FRANK. Maggie …
ANDREI. Florence …
JAMES. To be my wife …
FRANK and ANDREI. To be my wife …
LYNN, MAGGIE and MRS. KRAVITZ. To be my husband …
JAMES. Promising with divine assistance …
OTHERS. Promising with divine assistance …
JAMES. To be unto thee …
OTHERS. To be unto thee …
JAMES. A loving and faithful husband …
MAGGIE. A loving and faithful wife …
ANDREI. A loving / and faithful husband …
LYNN. A loving / and faithful wife …
FRANK. A loving / and faithful husband …
MRS. KRAVITZ. A loving and faithful wife …
JAMES and LYNN. So long as we both shall live.
ANDREI and MRS. KRAVITZ. So long as we both shall live.
FRANK and MAGGIE. So long as we both shall live. *(By the end of the vows, the music has swelled, the couples are seen only in silhouette, and the billboard glows on high — two figures, a full net of herring, and a leaky boat.)*

End of Play

PROPERTY LIST

Telephones
Sheets of paper
Coats
Shoe (FRANK, MAGGIE)
Envelope containing cruise tickets (FRANK)
Small box (JAMES)
Engagement ring (JAMES, LYNN, FRANK)
Library card (MAGGIE)
Change (MAGGIE)
Plastic bag (MAGGIE)
Notepad and pen (MAGGIE)
Police badge (MAGGIE)
Headphones (PETEY, FRANK)
Reel-to-reel tape recorder (PETEY)
Oats (MRS. McCARTHY)
Mixing bowl (MRS. McCARTHY)
Measuring cup (MRS. McCARTHY)
Clipboard with notes (MAGGIE)
Bubble-gum cigar (HARRY)
Mercury dime (HARRY, MAGGIE)
Album (MRS. KRAVITZ)
Army duffel (JAMES)
Paper bag (JAMES)
Box of Velveeta (JAMES, LYNN)
File of papers (MAGGIE, HARRY)
Keys (FRANK, MRS. KRAVITZ)
Passport (FRANK)
Election button (MAGGIE)
Bell (FRANK, MRS. VAN NOSTRAND)
Wedding veil (MRS. VAN NOSTRAND)
Flask (FRANK)
Marriage license (FRANK, CLERK)
Tea (HERBERT)
Shortbread (HERBERT)
Glasses of schnapps (HERBERT)
Tray (HERBERT)

Pistol (FRANK)
Laundry (MRS. KRAVITZ)
Shot glasses (ANDREI, BARTENDER)
Teaspoons (ANDREI, BARTENDER, MAGGIE)
Business card (MAGGIE, ANDREI)
Bait bucket and fishing gear (FRANK)
Handbag (LYNN)
Clipboard, stopwatch (DR. KASDEN)
Eye goggles (JAMES)
Shot glass in plastic bag (MAGGIE)
Metal canister (MAGGIE)
Shotgun (FRANK)
Handcuffs (FRANK)
White cane (JAMES)

SOUND EFFECTS

Phone ringing
Voice-over of commercial jingle
Hearings of the Senate Internal Security Subcommittee
Boat engine
Massive rumbling
Sound of man running into wooden pile
Splash

NOTE ON ALTERNATIVE TEXT

In order to accomodate setting constraints the following text may be substituted for that found between the asterisks on page 90.

LYNN. Over here, but — *
JAMES. I just want to hold you. *(He rushes toward the sound of her voice, misses completely and disappears offstage.)*
LYNN. Look out for the — *(There is the offstage "thunk!" of a man colliding with a wooden pile.)* James!
JAMES. *(O.S.)* I'm all right! *(James reenters, holding his head.)* I saw it, baby lamb. I saw the light. *
LYNN. Don't talk, darling, there are people here …

NOTE ON MUSIC

RED HERRING invites the use of short musical interludes to cover the many scene changes and to punctuate blackouts. Period "crime" music — squealing trumpets, melancholic saxophones, fast-walking basses, etc. — has been used to good effect following scenes that end with big plot twists. Likewise, various selections from Andrei's newest LP have been employed for comic effect or ironic commentary. Prospective producers should note, however, that it is incumbent upon them to obtain permission from copyright holders before using recorded music in any production of the play.

NEW PLAYS

★ **AGES OF THE MOON by Sam Shepard.** Byron and Ames are old friends, reunited by mutual desperation. Over bourbon on ice, they sit, reflect and bicker until fifty years of love, friendship and rivalry are put to the test at the barrel of a gun. "A poignant and honest continuation of themes that have always been present in the work of one of this country's most important dramatists, here reconsidered in the light and shadow of time passed." –NY Times. "Finely wrought...as enjoyable and enlightening as a night spent stargazing." –Talkin' Broadway. [2M] ISBN: 978-0-8222-2462-4

★ **ALL THE WAY by Robert Schenkkan. Winner of the 2014 Tony Award for Best Play.** November, 1963. An assassin's bullet catapults Lyndon Baines Johnson into the presidency. A Shakespearean figure of towering ambition and appetite, this charismatic, conflicted Texan hurls himself into the passage of the Civil Rights Act—a tinderbox issue emblematic of a divided America—even as he campaigns for re-election in his own right, and the recognition he so desperately wants. In Pulitzer Prize and Tony Award–winning Robert Schenkkan's vivid dramatization of LBJ's first year in office, means versus ends plays out on the precipice of modern America. ALL THE WAY is a searing, enthralling exploration of the morality of power. It's not personal, it's just politics. "...action-packed, thoroughly gripping... jaw-dropping political drama." –Variety. "A theatrical coup...nonstop action. The suspense of a first-class thriller." –NY1. [17M, 3W] ISBN: 978-0-8222-3181-3

★ **CHOIR BOY by Tarell Alvin McCraney.** The Charles R. Drew Prep School for Boys is dedicated to the creation of strong, ethical black men. Pharus wants nothing more than to take his rightful place as leader of the school's legendary gospel choir. Can he find his way inside the hallowed halls of this institution if he sings in his own key? "[An] affecting and honest portrait...of a gay youth tentatively beginning to find the courage to let the truth about himself become known." –NY Times. "In his stirring and stylishly told drama, Tarell Alvin McCraney cannily explores race and sexuality and the graces and gravity of history." –NY Daily News. [7M] ISBN: 978-0-8222-3116-5

★ **THE ELECTRIC BABY by Stefanie Zadravec.** When Helen causes a car accident that kills a young man, a group of fractured souls cross paths and connect around a mysterious dying baby who glows like the moon. Folk tales and folklore weave throughout this magical story of sad endings, strange beginnings and the unlikely people that get you from one place to the next. "The imperceptible magic that pervades human existence and the power of myth to assuage sorrow are invoked by the playwright as she entwines the lives of strangers in THE ELECTRIC BABY, a touching drama." –NY Times. "As dazzling as the dialogue is dreamful." –Pittsburgh City Paper. [3M, 3W] ISBN: 978-0-8222-3011-3

DRAMATISTS PLAY SERVICE, INC.
440 Park Avenue South, New York, NY 10016 212-683-8960 Fax 212-213-1539
postmaster@dramatists.com www.dramatists.com